Getting into Teacher Education: a Handbook

Vinicius NOBRE
Catarina PONTES

CENGAGE
Learning®

Austrália • Brasil • Coreia • Espanha • Estados Unidos • Japão • México • Reino Unido • Cingapura

CENGAGE
Learning

Getting into Teacher Education: a Handbook
Vinicius Nobre and Catarina Pontes

Gerente editorial: Noelma Brocanelli

Gerente de projetos especiais: Luciana Rabuffetti

Supervisora de produção gráfica: Fabiana Alencar Albuquerque

Editora de desenvolvimento: Regina Helena Madureira Plascak

Editora de aquisições: Guacira Simonelli

Assistente editorial: Joelma Andrade

Editor: Juan Pablo Rodríguez Velázquez

Revisão: Francisco Lozano González

Diagramação: Alma Soto Zárraga / MB Soluciones Editoriales México

Capa: Alma Soto Zárraga e Luis Angel Arreguín/ MB Soluciones Editoriales México

Pesquisa Iconográfica: ABMM Pesquisa Iconográfica

Imagem da capa: vs148/Shutterstock.com

Impresso no Brasil.
Printed in Brazil.
1 2 3 4 5 6   19 18 17

Para informações sobre nossos produtos, entre em contato pelo telefone 0800 11 19 39

Para permissão de uso de material desta obra, envie seu pedido para **direitosautorais@cengage.com**

© 2017 Cengage Learning. Todos os direitos reservados.

ISBN-13: 978-85-221-2552-4
ISBN-10: 85-221-2552-X

Cengage Learning
Condomínio E-Business Park
Rua Werner Siemens, 111 – Prédio 11 – Torre A – Conjunto 12
Lapa de Baixo – CEP 05069-900
São Paulo – SP
Tel.: (11) 3665-9900 – Fax: (11) 3665-9901
SAC: 0800 11 19 39

Para suas soluções de curso e aprendizado, visite
www.cengage.com.br

Dados Internacionais de Catalogação na Publicação (CIP)
(Câmara Brasileira do Livro, SP, Brasil)

N754g Nobre, Vinicius.
   Getting into teacher education : a handbook / Vinicius Nobre, Catarina Pontes. – São Paulo, SP : Cengage Learning, 2016. 104 p. : il., 26 cm.

Inclui bibliografia
ISBN 978-85-221-2552-4

1. Professor de inglês – Formação. 2. Professores de inglês – Manuais, guias etc. I. Pontes, Catarina. II. Título.

CDU 371-13:802.0   CDU-370.71

Índices para catálogo sistemático:

1. Professor de inglês – Formação   371.13:802.0
(Bibliotecária responsável: Sabrina Leal Araujo – CRB 10/1507)

index

Vinicius Nobre is the Academic Manager of Associação Cultura Inglesa São Paulo. He has been involved with English Language Teaching, Teacher Education, Course Design, Exam Boards and Education Management for several years. He is past president of BRAZ-TESOL and has had the opportunity to work as a CELTA and ICELT assessor/ moderator, Cambridge Examiner/ Team Leader, DELTA tutor and course book writer. He is passionate about people development in every possible way and hopes to contribute to a greater level of professionalization in the EFL teaching career.

Catarina Pontes is an Academic Coordinator at Associação Cultura Inglesa São Paulo. She has been involved with English Language Teaching, Teacher Training, Course Design, and International Exams for several years. She is an ICELT tutor, a Cambridge English Language Assessment Speaking Examiner and Team Leader, has published articles In ELT and EFL, contributed to ELT blogs and presented at international conferences. She has been involved with Braz-TESOL and is currently a member of IATEFL's Pronunciation SIG.

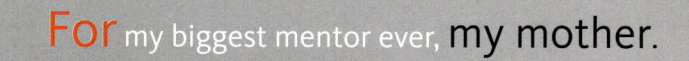

For my biggest mentor ever, **my mother.**

(Vinnie)

For my loving parents Luiz and Neusa – who taught me the importance of education;
For my beloved son Rafael – my pride and joy;
For my dearest Vinnie– mentor, friend, and partner in crime.

(Catarina)

Acknowledgements

We have only been able to write this book due to of the incredible support of the institution we work for. Most of our learning, experiences and professional growth have been made possible because we work in an organization that encourages continuous development and inspires us to always go the extra mile. We would like to thank all of our colleagues in the Academic Department of Cultura Inglesa São Paulo for their ideas, critique and companionship. We would also like to thank Lizika Goldchleger, our reference of excellence, professionalism and hard work. We have to award a special mention to Lorraine de Matos, our CEO and one of the most inspiring professionals we have met. Not only did she allow us to accept so many challenges (including writing this book) but she also pushed us restlessly and celebrated every single achievement.

Our dear friends from Cengage Learning, who invited us to write this book using extremely convincing techniques and who always believed in our potential, deserve our immense gratitude. Finally, we need to thank all the teacher trainers, educators, mentors and peers that we have had throughout these years. The list is very long and we do not want to run the risk of forgetting to mention someone. But we are thankful to everyone that you has shared with us so much of their time, knowledge and experience, turning us into these mosaics called Catarina Pontes and Vinicius Nobre, two completely different patchworks of professional lives that have found in each other new elements that complete, tease, challenge and enrich us.

Preface

Even though both of us had always dreamed of a career as teacher educators, we actually got involved with developing English language teachers by accident. Therefore, due to our organic venture into something so new, a lot of our more immediate learning ended up coming from the amazing trainers we met—as opposed to formal courses or complex readings. We were privileged to work with experienced professionals who took the time to mentor and guide us so that we could become better able to work with the most diverse practitioners. Not everyone is as lucky as we were to find such support when embracing new challenges in teacher education. It was through trial and error, and plenty of feedback, that we improved our sessions, workshops, feedback meetings and courses, until we had built up the courage to delve into more academic bibliography about teacher development. There are already plenty of books on the topic and a lot of research has been carried out. However, it all seemed a bit too intimidating when we first started. We had recently stepped into the world of teacher training with little formal education on how to do it and feared that some of the literature on the topic would be slightly out of reach for us, beginners in the career.

This book aims at bridging this gap. We want to provide experienced teachers (and trainers who have just started working with English teachers) a more straightforward and practical handbook to help them deal with this new role. Our book should help those who never had any support to transition into the role of "trainer" but should also bring something new to the lucky professionals who have had an experienced someone by their side to coach them into becoming a "trainer". We are fully aware, however, that in this book we have only provided a bird's eye view of all that there is in teacher education. We have only touched on some themes that certainly deserve a much more in-depth analysis and exploration. Nevertheless, our goal here is not ambitious; it is to simply introduce some concepts, present fundamental guidelines and generate interest to empower the future generations of teacher trainers to go after further knowledge, more comprehensive materials and up-to-date research. We have also used some terms interchangeably in order to be coherent with our proposal of writing a practical and dynamic handbook. Hence, it is important to reinforce that we do not assume "teacher training", "teacher development", "teacher education", "coaching" or "mentoring" should be considered synonymous by scholars and experts, for example. In the context of this book, we have consciously avoided more sensitive (and sometimes controversial) definitions of each of these terms in order to maintain a fast-paced introductory reading that focuses on what we thought would be more relevant to our readers at this point.

Finally, the whole process of writing this book has been an amazing journey of reflection upon our own careers, our practice and an opportunity to think of how we can grow as professionals. We truly hope our thoughts and ideas might prompt you to embark on a similar journey towards a career that we have been in love with for so long.

Vinicius Nobre and Catarina Pontes

Visit this book website at www.cengage.com.br to access this textbook in Portuguese.

C hapter 1

Getting into teacher training and teacher supervision

"Many language teachers often wonder about the different possibilities that the career may offer. An experienced teacher might become involved with material design, research on language acquisition, distance learning, education management, or teacher training, among other things. Often, the transition to these different positions happens in a rather organic, meandering fashion, which may pose a challenge to professionals who aspire to climb the career ladder. Their recurring question is: "How do I get started?"."

© Halfpoint/Shutterstock.com

Many language teachers often wonder about the different possibilities that the career may offer. An experienced teacher might get involved with material design, research on language acquisition, distance learning, education management, or teacher training, among other things. Often, the transition to these different positions happens in a rather organic, meandering fashion, which may pose a challenge to professionals who aspire to climb the career ladder. Their recurring question is: "How do I get started?".

There are very few courses and not much literature on the actual process of embarking on any of these waters (which resembles the nature of teaching). Teaching is often considered a rather erratic profession and the difficulty of systematising a path for one's own development in order to embrace new activities in Teaching English as a Foreign Language (TEFL) might be even greater when it comes to educating other teachers. Freeman (1989: 27), for instance, says that "language teacher education has become increasingly fragmented and unfocused. Based on a kaleidoscope of elements from many disciplines, efforts to educate individuals as language teachers often lack a coherent, commonly accepted foundation. In its place, teacher educators and teacher education programs substitute their own individual rationales, based on pedagogical assumptions or research, or function in a vacuum, assuming—yet never articulating—the bases from which they work." This scenario might make the task of becoming a trainer a hard one to accomplish.

Nonetheless, many professionals still wish to follow this route. The job of a teacher—no matter how creative or varied it may be across the years—still presents an element of predictability in its goals and routine. Becoming a teacher trainer is sometimes perceived as a natural option to get out of a certain rut. Not always, however, is the stimulus for this desire based on the knowledge of what the role demands and entails.

For the professionals who still aim at training others, after having understood the scope of the activity itself (which is exactly what we aim to present in this book), Beaven (2004) suggests some possible ways to get into teacher training. She says that you might: (1) be asked by someone to do it, (2) get a job where training is expected of you, (3) ask an organization if they will let you become a trainer, or (4) find a mentor who will gradually guide you into teacher training. From our experience, you are more likely to get into training "by accident" than getting into it because you actually applied for the position. Competent teachers with a mature attitude, qualifications, and the seniority to educate other professionals can be hard to find. When an organization, or a more senior trainer, runs into someone who presents these competencies that are required of a good trainer, the invitation is inevitable. There are still obstacles in the process that are not often shared, nevertheless. One of the most difficult obstacles (often unknown to many) is that as one moves on to become responsible for other

> ...professionals need to consider the different skills that they will have to consolidate, master, or develop while training others.

people's development, their relationships and responsibilities will have to change significantly. For example, the way they are perceived by their community, the way they come across, the weight of the decisions they make, and the pressure added to their teaching practice will also change. As you accept a new post, new values, skills, priorities, demands, and reach of actions have to be acknowledged. The impact of your every action is more profound, and it has to be. What sometimes happens is that the (pseudo) glamour of being a trainer overshadows the hardships of the role and professionals getting into teacher education for the first time might be faced with the deconstruction of the illusion that it is easy. It is therefore very important to highlight that as you become a trainer, your challenges will be new and very different from what you used to do in the classroom.

Training teachers is not the same as teaching language students. Some might think that if they were successful as teachers they will be successful trainers because instead of teaching kids, for instance, they will be teaching teachers. Unfortunately, this is not true. There is much more to educating professionals than there is in the art of teaching a foreign language. It is crucial to understand that as a trainer you can really influence people's careers—you might have the power to inspire them to aim higher or even the power to make them fall out of love with teaching and learning.

Moreover, new trainers often disregard the fact that as you go up to a higher position, you will naturally become lonelier whether you work for an institution or as a freelancer. It is naïve to imagine that the weight of your decisions, the confidentiality of what you hear and see, and the direct interaction with directors of studies, policy makers, and other new stakeholders will not result in you and "your old crowd" drifting apart. You will go from being a peer to being a more senior representative of an organisation. What you say to other professionals will be associated with the voice of the company you represent and your actions will determine the model to be followed by others. Few teachers who wish to get into teacher training are aware of these issues and, likewise, few leaders communicate the less appealing side of the role. Not being able to cope with greater accountability and heavier responsibilities is what usually frustrates new trainers.

Being aware of what the job has in store for you (the laurels and the obstacles) is essential for making an informed decision about the future and having a down-to-earth start in the career.

> Teachers can be effective practitioners without necessarily being fully aware of the principles they work by...

After being invited to act as a trainer and having weighed the pros and cons of being a teacher educator, professionals need to consider the different skills that they will have to consolidate, master, or develop while training others. As we mentioned before, being a teacher educator is not the same as educating language learners; although some competencies are quite similar, trainers are expected to master them more comfortably and develop new ones as well. For example, even though in both cases you will need skills of empathy and understanding, when teaching you may use a variety of questioning techniques to apply these skills; in training you will need to go beyond that.

As a trainer, you will use these techniques in order to get people to develop a line of reasoning so that they can identify and reflect upon the inconsistencies in their own beliefs, which is quite a leap from the kind of work done by language teachers with their groups. Another skill that trainers have to present that may not be expected from teachers is a very conscious knowledge of what goes on in the classroom and a very formal understanding of the processes of teaching and learning foreign languages.

Teachers can be effective practitioners without necessarily being fully aware of the principles they work by; trainers, on the other hand, need to display a solid theoretical background that will enable them to justify, exemplify, and expand their and others' actual practice. Another important aspect to be taken into account is that the results of your actions will take longer to become evident.

As a teacher, you can witness learners developing their linguistic skills more quickly; as a trainer, however, it might be a while before you see teachers develop a wider range of classroom techniques and improve their teaching skills. Therefore, trainers need to adjust their own expectations regarding the outcomes of the people they are working with. They are less likely to show achievements at the same speed that language learners will.

The relationship with other professionals can also be more complex than the relationship teachers build with language learners. Beaven (2004), for example, states that trainers need people skills of a higher order since one of the biggest challenges of educating other teachers is realising that they may not be willing to import into their own classrooms what they experience in training sessions.

Trainers will then have to develop skills in order to help teachers want to learn in a collaborative environment, becoming more aware and open. Dealing with the issue of how to

> ...you do not become a teacher trainer to get away from the classroom, but because you love the classroom environment.

relate to teachers in order to trigger development—under possibly less favourable conditions—can sound intimidating, especially when you need to train, educate, and develop people who used to be your peers just a while before. In order to manage it more smoothly, it is important to consider the level of formality in the interpersonal climate between advisor and advisee as suggested by Randall and Thornton (2001: 9). They say that "the provision of effective advice depends to a large degree on the perceived status of the advisor by the advisee and the consequent interpersonal 'distance' between them." They claim that a trainer needs to be aware of the potential constraints that interpersonal and cultural factors might have on the relationship with trainees and work towards counteracting them.

The people skills required to assess the interpersonal climate with trainees, to promote the willingness to change, and to maintain a professional distance without jeopardizing trust are of paramount importance as new trainers venture into teacher education.

All in all, what will lead you to become a successful teacher trainer is your passion for teaching and learning, your drive to help teachers promote learning and foster independence in their students, and your constant pursuit of professional development. If you are trying to avoid the classroom, we regret having to tell you this is not the career move you are looking for—you do not become a teacher trainer to get away from the classroom, but because you love the classroom environment.

References:

Beaven, B. (2004) *How Eight English Language Teacher Trainers Made the Transition From Teaching to Training.* Unpublished dissertation. Exeter: The University of Exeter.

Freeman, D. (1989) *Teacher Training, Development, and Decision Making: A Model of Teaching and Related Strategies for Language Teacher Education.* In TESOL Quarterly Volume 23, number 1 (mar,1989).

Randall, M. & Thornton, B. (2001) *Advising and supporting teachers.* Cambridge: Cambridge University Press.

Tasks for Chapter 1

Task 1
A questionnaire: Am I ready to become a teacher trainer?

Getting into teacher training can be very exciting, but quite daunting, too. It is vital for the trainer-to-be to become extremely aware of the competencies they already have and to be able to identify the gaps that need to be bridged. If you are considering getting into teacher training, perhaps the following questions might shed some light on how well prepared you are, as well as help you analyse your strengths and weaknesses. Take some time to go through them carefully. When you have finished, consider designing a plan of action to focus on the competencies you need to develop (see Table 1.1).

Task 2
Videorecording your lesson

Before setting out to help novice (or even experienced) teachers, a trainer should (1) be able to identify what it is that makes their lesson a model to be followed, and (2) should be well aware of the aspects that they need to work on in order to provide trainees with sound reference of good teaching practice. A trainer should then first wear their teacher's hat and find the resources and/or tools to spot the above-mentioned aspects and come up with an action plan to work on the areas in their own lessons that need improvement and further development. It is of paramount importance for a trainer to first be able to identify their own strengths and weaknesses when teaching, and only then move on to guide and educate fellow teachers.

Videorecording your lesson is one of the ways to help you identify your strengths and weaknesses as a teacher, and it can be an invaluable experience – you may be able to spot things you say in class you had never imagined you do (e.g., an overuse of questions such as *OK?* or *Yes* or *No?*), learn about how you react to learners' contributions with facial expressions, identify blind spots and even notice how learners react or behave during the lesson when you turn to face the board, for example. Moreover, after having answered the questionnaire (see Table 1.2), you might be able to gain even further insight to help you answer some of the questions and have more concrete evidence to help you with your plan of action.

You can decide whether you want to videorecord only your delivery of the lesson (thus having the camera focusing on you the whole lesson), or videorecord you and the learners (and ask someone else to help you with the videoing). In the second case, you should ask learners to sign a document giving you permission to videorecord them (in the case of underage learners, parents should be contacted). Your choice here will depend on your purpose for videoing the lesson. Raising your awareness of your own delivery will enable you to help the teachers you are training.

Table 1.1

1	• How long have I been teaching English for? • In which contexts have I taught the language (e.g. EFL, ESL, ESP)?	
2	• Have I always worked at the same institution or for different ones? • What does this experience tell me?	
3	• Have I taught a wide range of levels and ages? • If so, which ones do I have more experience with? • If not, how am I planning to become more familiar with the levels and ages I do not have much experience with?	
4	• Am I familiar with different methods and approaches to teaching EFL? • Which ones am I more used to? Which ones should I learn more about?	
5	• Which teaching qualifications have I already got? Which should be the next ones I acquire?	
6	• Am I ready to cope with a position as a trainer? • Does my community recognise me as a good candidate for that position? Why (not)?	
7	• Am I aware of what this change of roles entails (from teacher to teacher trainer)? • Do I know the challenges that teacher training brings? • Am I willing to cope with them?	
8	• Which skills have I already got that can be adapted to being a teacher trainer? Which ones do I need to develop?	

...the pursuit of continuous professional development is key in any profession.

The following chart can be used when you are watching your videoed lesson and can also inform your action plan:

Table 1.2

1.	What do I identify as strengths in my lesson?	
2.	What do I identify as weaknesses in my lesson?	
3.	What do I learn from learners' reactions?	
4.	Am I a good linguistic model for my learners?	
5.	What could a trainee teacher learn from observing my lesson? (i.e., which good teaching practices do you have?)	

© Nobre & Pontes

If you had a peer teacher videorecord your lesson, you could also ask them for some feedback based on the points you identified in the chart above. Use your notes and answers for the questions above to inform your next steps for development.

Task 3
Devising an action plan for development

The pursuit of continuous professional development is key in any profession. In the field of English Language Teaching (ELT), it is important not only to keep up-to-date with methods and approaches to teaching, but also to keep on improving your knowledge about language and teaching.

Having answered the questionnaire in Task 2 and having been able to learn more about your practice with the videoed lesson, it is crucial for you to devise an action plan that will keep you on the path of continuous professional development.

Using the information you have gathered in the previous tasks, devise an action plan for your development as a teacher of teachers. It is crucial for you to be a model for the teachers you are going to train, and being able to identify the areas in which you need to improve is essential. Moreover, your objectives should be SMART – Specific (you need a clear focus), Measurable (you need to collect evidence), Achievable (do not aim too high), Realistic (take into account all your other routine activities) and Time-bound (set yourself a deadline). With this concept in mind, you stand better chances of achieving your objectives and taking the next steps in your professional development.

The frame we suggest below is aimed at helping you devise your action plan:

> I would like to improve my (teaching skills or knowledge about language) because I have realised in my videoed lesson that (reason for focusing on the previously mentioned issue) and I do not think this is a good model for the teachers I am going to train. In order to achieve my objective, I am willing to (describe what you have considered doing) (state how often (once a week, for instance)) and by (state a deadline), I hope to have become better able to (refer to main aim).

© Nobre & Pontes

Chapter 2

Approaches to teacher training

"This chapter aims at highlighting and looking into possible approaches to be taken when devising teacher training and professional development initiatives. We are first going to justify the importance of consciously choosing a framework for training, then discuss two tools that can be used to inform this decision (the KASA framework and the Johari Window), and will wrap up by suggesting some training processes and approaches that trainers can appeal to in order to maximise the potential of their efforts towards training."

© ImageFlow/Shutterstock.com

Often times, training is planned organically, resorting merely to the trainer's previous experience and failing to rely on a more structured framework. This informality might prevent good ideas from being better and more professionally explored. Likewise, training courses frequently tend to focus on rather technical and mechanical aspects of the job, not giving trainee teachers a very clear picture of their role and what they are likely to run into, which might eventually lead to rather high rates of staff turnover as expectations might not have been aligned from the start.

Woodward (2005) also mentions a tendency for training courses to be underfunded and happen in fewer days, especially because of the high demand for teachers in the market. All of these variables have to be taken into account when managing other people's professional growth. Planning training initiatives, designing entire training courses or simply preparing a couple of workshops that intend to foster professional development can be more challenging and complex than many institutions and novice trainers would like to believe. Careful research and formal knowledge about the processes of training are vital.

As a first step, we would like to suggest some questions to be asked right at the start of any teacher education process that should help trainers decide on the most appropriate approach or framework:

1. What is the profile of my trainees? Are they novice or experienced teachers?

2. What are my goals as a trainer? My institution's goals? My trainees' goals?

3. What are the overall expected outcomes of this training initiative?

4. How much time can my trainees invest in this training course?

5. What resources will I have access to? What about resources for trainees?

After getting a more detailed view of the context, we can move on to the drawing board. However, before rushing into choosing the content of sessions or determining the timetable, it is very important to make sure trainers share clear beliefs and views regarding their role and the expected goals of the process. These views and beliefs together with the answers to the questions above should underlie the selection of the content of sessions, the organisation of the work to be done, the prioritisation of input, and the ratio between practice and theory, and should be mirrored in tutors' attitudes and behavior in a consistent manner. In summary, it is crucial for trainers to have a view of language teaching and one of how to educate teachers for their job (Freeman, 1989).

In order to get more detailed answers to the five questions above—and before deciding on which approach to resort to—it is important for trainers to assess and evaluate what trainees already know so that choices are more informed, materials are better chosen and time is better spent throughout the training initiative. A good starting point to diagnose needs and areas for improvement can be Freeman's (1989) KASA (*Knowledge, Awareness, Skills* and *Attitude*) framework.

This very comprehensive framework can be of great help to structure development programs and raise awareness of gaps in competencies. In addition, these four aspects are of considerable help not only throughout one specific training course. They can be the main pillars for a continuous awareness-raising exercise that can inform the long-term planning of training initiatives. We shall look at these aspects in further detail below.

Knowledge and Skills can be considered the most technical aspects of the framework, being more easily measured and identified, whereas Awareness and Attitude are less obvious and more behavioural, thus more subjective areas. Professionals that present a balance of the four constituents certainly stand better chances of success in the job market. Likewise, trainers who aim at helping teachers develop all four characteristics are more likely to promote more complete growth. In general terms, the KASA framework can be described as follows:

- Knowledge entails teachers' knowledge about language teaching and learning— language systems and skills, language acquisition, teaching methodology and assessment, learning styles and the contexts in which the teaching will occur— sociocultural, institutional and situational (Freeman, 1989), among other factors. It is also crucial that teachers maintain up-to-date knowledge about the above-mentioned features.

- Awareness refers to the ability to acknowledge and keep track of the attention one gives or is giving to something. It is about knowing your areas for improvement, and being willing to work on them—be they related to technical knowledge (about language or teaching, for instance), or a more behavioural aspect (such as people skills). Some questions trainers may want to ask teachers might include, "Are you aware of how you react to learners' contributions?", "Are you aware of how much learners have spoken in your lesson?", and "Are you aware of the impact/influence your comments can have on a learner?"

- Skills refer, more specifically, to the aspects related to the delivery of the lesson—presenting materials, giving clear instructions and teaching language, of course. Further examples include your classroom management techniques, your ability with technology (dealing with possible technical difficulties in a lesson, for instance), dealing with discipline issues in a lesson, and knowing how to teach learning strategies successfully.

- Attitude, as Freeman (1989) states, "is an interplay of externally oriented behaviour, actions and perceptions on the one hand, and internal intrapersonal dynamics, feelings and reactions on the other." It is your reaction, for example, to constructive feedback, how you greet a latecomer into your lesson, how you feel towards individual learners, and how much of a team member you are.

When devising training initiatives, trainers should consider whether they intend to focus on all of these four elements or privilege some. In general terms, the focus tends to be very often on the more technical aspects (Knowledge and Skills). However, trainers might be overlooking two very impactful competencies to be considered when training a professional who will deal with education. However hard it may be to tackle Attitude and Awareness, the benefits of taking them into account when planning teacher education are quite significant. Neglecting these more behavioural aspects, on the other hand, can cost the institution dearly and, even worse, might have a negative impact on a learner's classroom experience. It is very important that trainers identify behavioural attitude that is not adequate to the role of a teacher and take the best action whenever possible.

Professionals might have sound technical knowledge but lack awareness of what they need to improve, for example, or display attitude issues that will interfere negatively in their development and ultimately in students' experience. Ideally, a skilled professional will have a good balance of formal knowledge, awareness of competencies and the areas s/he needs to work on in order to bridge his/her competency gaps, and the right attitude to pursue professional development. Ideally, trainers should aim at helping professionals develop holistically. The KASA framework is, therefore, one of a number of tools that trainers can resort to in order to start designing a thorough training course and to assess candidates' performance. Based on the identified strengths and weaknesses, trainers can make more informed decisions and generate better results.

Another effective tool trainers can make use of is the *Johari window*. Named after the two psychologists who came up with the technique in 1955—Joseph Luft and Harrington Ingham—the idea is to invite teachers on a journey of self-awareness, one by the end of which they will be better able to understand their relationship with themselves and with others (colleagues and personal relations as well). Just like the KASA framework, this analysis might provide trainers and trainees with precious information that can be used in favour of professional development.

The window has four quadrants, with each of them representing a different aspect of the "self." A representation of the window can be found below:

1 Known Self Things we know about ourselves and others know about us.	2 Hidden Self Things we know about ourselves and others do not know.
3 Blind Self Things others know about us and we do not know.	4 Unknown Self Things neither we nor others know about us.

(Adapted from http://www.designedalliance.com/reflections-in-your-johari-window/)

Area 1 is also known as the "area of free activity." This is the information about the person that is shared between the person and others—behaviour, attitude, feelings, emotion, knowledge, experience, skills, views, etc. When we work in this area with others we are likely to be at our most effective and productive because this is the space where good communication and cooperation occur, free from distractions, mistrust, confusion, conflict, and misunderstanding. Professionals can learn more about themselves in order to expand the size of their open area by seeking and actively listening to feedback. This process is known as "feedback solicitation." Trainers can play an important role in facilitating feedback and disclosure among group members, and in directly giving feedback to individuals about their own blind areas. If feedback is carried out successfully, trainers will be able to promote a culture of open, helpful, constructive, and sensitive communication, which might favour the sharing of knowledge among teachers and institutions.

Area 2 refers to everything that is known about a person by others, but is unknown by the person him/herself. As mentioned previously, honest feedback from others should reduce this area and increase the open area; this exercise will naturally increase self-awareness. This blind area is not an effective space for individuals or groups because it may include issues in which one is deluded or issues that others are deliberately withholding from a person. Being in the dark will prevent teachers from focusing on key areas for improvement or prioritising developmental needs. Trainers have some responsibility for helping teachers to reduce their blind area by giving genuine and constructive feedback. Teacher educators should promote an environment of disclosure and non-judgmental feedback, which will eventually reduce fear and consequently help professionals build self-confidence and trust.

Area 3 is what is known to ourselves but unknown to others. This hidden self represents information, feelings, or whatever a person knows about themselves but is not revealed. This area might also include reservations, fears, hidden agendas, and secrets. Personal and private information usually remains hidden, which is absolutely fine since certain feelings and experiences have no bearing on the act of teaching. However, a lot of hidden information is work- or performance-related. In these situations, professionals will benefit from positioning this information in the open area. Trainers can encourage teachers to tell others how they feel and other information about themselves in order to reduce this hidden area, and therefore increase the open area. This practice might enable better understanding, cooperation, sympathy, and teamwork.

In area 4 we are going to find aptitudes, information, feelings, latent abilities, and experiences that are unknown to the self and to others. These unknown issues can be quite close to the surface, and might be positive and useful. However, sometimes they can be deeper aspects of a person's personality that influence behaviour to various degrees. Through self-discovery or observation by others, teachers might learn more about themselves and get in contact with this information of which they are unaware. In order to help trainees reduce their own unknown area, trainers can also provide them with the opportunity to experiment with new things, techniques, tasks and methods with no great pressure to succeed. Trainers can also help by creating an environment that encourages self-discovery, and by promoting the processes of constructive observation and feedback among fellow teachers.

Both the KASA framework and the *Johari window* can be used as tools to learn more about teachers (whether novice or experienced) before the start of a training program but also during the implementation of a course. They are powerful tools that aim at raising awareness and informing decisions.

After learning more about the profile of the trainees, it is very important to reflect upon the structure of a training process. McGrath (1997) describes four "modes" of teaching and learning and "process options." He states that oftentimes the course objective determines the course content and processes are then selected. What he suggests, and we entirely agree with, is that the objective should inform both the content and the selection of the process. The selected mode should clearly relate to the main objective and trainers, due to the seniority of their role, should be able to justify and be explicit about the decisions they make.

McGrath presents four categories: Feeding, Leading, Throwing and Showing (as in the illustration below).

	Knowing	
	FEEDING lecture reading	**LEADING** Socratic questioning awareness-raising tasks
Teacher *Centred*		*Learner* *Centred*
	SHOWING demonstration 'mirroring'	**THROWING** teaching practice workshop
	Doing	

(McGrath, 1997)

We are going to very briefly define these four categories:

Feeding – the direct transmission of information or opinion about the language, teaching, or a relevant theoretical discipline. Trainers can "feed" through the spoken word (lecture, presentations) or written texts (hand-outs, readings). This is a rather economical and effective way to provide an audience with an introduction or an overview of a given topic, despite being potentially tedious and not necessarily serving as a good example of teaching practice.

Leading – the process by which course participants are guided towards knowledge or awareness or towards a conscious or analytical understanding of what they already "know." Even though it might be more time-consuming, this approach favours a more learner-centred experience and allows teachers to arrive at their own conclusions through eliciting and awareness-raising activities.

Showing – the provision of models or examples of language, for instance, or teaching techniques. The objective of this approach is to provide concrete examples and models that teachers can later resort to. McGrath warns us that we need to be aware "that, if unfamiliar, they may not become part of a participant's repertoire unless we also provide opportunities for sheltered practice (and feedback)."

Throwing – the exposition of participants to the realities of everyday life, in real or simulated situations, giving them an opportunity to perform one or other of the roles associated with teaching. In this approach, trainees actually do things—they rehearse and they learn and get better by doing.

McGrath (1997) quotes Richards and Rodgers (1986) to say that,

> "It has been suggested that every language teacher operates with a theory of language and a theory of learning, normally assumptions and beliefs. It should therefore follow that every teacher trainer also operates with theories, among them a theory of learning. One difference between teachers and teacher trainers is that the latter are normally expected to be capable of being explicit about their theories."

However, from our experience, when starting in the field of teacher training, professionals might be unaware of the theories regarding teacher education (such as McGrath's four categories) and might end up designing training programs without necessarily being able to justify why they make certain choices. This fairly straightforward organisation of four

> In this chapter we wanted to offer a brief introduction to the practical aspects in devising training courses and sessions.

modes should help new trainers reflect upon which approaches to use and when, striking a reasonable balance and considering the profile of their trainees in order to become more effective and productive.

In this chapter, we wanted to offer a brief introduction to the practical aspects in devising training courses and sessions. We started by pointing out that training teachers is different from teaching language learners and the techniques, strategies, and approaches used should come from the field of teacher education. We also emphasised the importance of having trainers become more aware of their role and the processes that they select. We then discussed two tools that can be used in order to investigate trainees' needs, competencies, profile, and abilities; and that might also be referred to throughout one's professional life. Finally, we very briefly outlined four macro categories that can inform trainers and help them design training initiatives, while bearing in mind the process being used and the expected outcome.

References:

Freeman, D. (1989) Teacher Training, Development, and Decision Making: A Model of Teaching and Related Strategies for Language Teacher Education. In *TESOL Quarterly* Volume 23, number 1.

Luft, J. and Ingham, H. (1955) *The Johari Window: a Graphic Model for Interpersonal Relations.* University of California Western Training Lab.

McGrath, I. (1997) Feeding, Leading, Showing, Throwing: Process choices in Teacher Training and Trainer Training. In *ELTRS: Learning to Train (Perspectives on the Development of Language Teacher Trainers).* Hemel Hempstead: Prentice Hall.

Richards, J. and Rodgers, T. (1986) *Approaches and Methods in Language Teaching.* Cambridge: CUP.

Woodward, T. (2005) *Ways of Working with Teachers.* Kent: Tessa Woodward Publications.

Tasks for Chapter 2

Task 1
Working on your KASA framework

In this chapter, we referred to Freeman's (1989) KASA framework and how implementing it can inform training initiatives. Being aware of our own strengths and weaknesses with regard to our Knowledge, Awareness, Skills and Attitudes should shed some light on the competencies we already have and help us focus on the areas for development and improvement. Fill in the frame below as an awareness exercise thinking of your abilities as both a teacher and as a trainer, focusing on your competencies in the KASA framework. Using this frame as a reflection exercise can inform you of your strong areas and of the ones you need to dedicate more time to developing. Please refer back to Chapter 2 in order to cover all areas under the four aspects in the framework.

The same grid can then be used with trainee teachers — you will just need to remove the "trainer" column. See Table 2.1.

Task 2
Developing your awareness – using the Johari window

In Chapter 2, we described the *Johari window* (term coined by Joseph Luft and Harrington Ingham), a tool that can be immensely helpful in informing trainers of trainees' level of awareness regarding their competencies, and also of the relationship they have with themselves and with others.

Our suggestion for this task is the following: invite a peer to observe your lesson. At the end of the lesson, reflect upon the delivery and take notes that can help you with the aspects covered in the Johari window. Get together with your peer and ask questions that can help you become more aware of your attitude and behaviour in the classroom, for instance. As a follow-up, consider listing ways in which you can improve as a teacher and become a role model as a trainer. Please revisit Chapter 2 for further details on each of the four quadrants (see Table 2.2). Quadrant four might end up being blank because of its very nature.

Table 2.1

	As a Teacher		As a trainer
	Strengths	Weaknesses	Development Needs
K Knowledge			
A Awareness			
S Skills			
A Attitude			

© Nobre & Pontes

Table 2.2

1 **Known Self**	2 **Hidden Self**
3 **Blind Self**	4 **Unknown Self**

(Adaptation of the Johari window by Nobre & Pontes)

> ...you can make a more informed decision as to which activities/category will better suit your trainees' needs.

Summarise your overall strengths and weaknesses in the chart below, suggesting a plan of action and achievable deadlines.

Overall strengths	
Overall weaknesses	
Plan of action	
Deadlines	

© Nobre & Pontes

Task 3
Feeding, Leading, Showing or Throwing?

The process categories described in Chapter 2, namely Feeding, Leading, Showing, and Throwing, aim at informing a trainer of the most effective ways to conduct a training course. Based on your trainees' competencies, needs, and areas for improvement, you will be able to design your course so that you provide them with the best tools for development. Time constraints and unexpected institutional needs may also play an important role in the process categories chosen for the training course to be delivered.

In order to make informed choices to meet your trainees' needs, you may want to keep track of all the information they share with you in the pre-course interviews and tests. This invaluable information should help you decide whether trainees will need more hands-on practice throughout the course, or if they need more theoretical input sessions.

Refer to the types of activities suggested for each category in Chapter 2, and think of possible advantages and disadvantages for them. By listing the possible strengths and weaknesses for each category, you can make a more informed decision as to which activities/category will better suit your trainees' needs.

Table 2.3

Feeding		Leading	
Advantages	Disadvantages	Advantages	Disadvantages
Showing		Throwing	
Advantages	Disadvantages	Advantages	Disadvantages

Chapter 3

Planning lessons with novice teachers

"Lesson planning means you respect your learners and you want to be as prepared as possible to provide them with a pleasant and memorable learning experience. In this chapter, we are going to focus on the trainer's role in helping teachers (both novice and experienced) understand the importance of lesson planning and offering support through the analysis, discussion and reflection that can be triggered by the exercise of putting ideas onto paper."

As we have mentioned previously, many teachers often start their career in a meandering manner, learning from experience and walking into a classroom with little (if any) formal training. We have met several teachers with a number of years of experience who started teaching in a more organic way and ended up developing strategies to manage their groups, memorising activities and creating their own materials and resources based on experience. All of this can be done without teachers having ever written a real plan. However, our experience has shown us that lesson planning is an extremely valuable tool to develop practitioners and increase the quality of their work. Scrivener (2011) states that "planning is essentially a thinking skill... It involves prediction, anticipation, sequencing, organising and simplifying." Lesson planning means you respect your learners and you want to be as prepared as possible to provide them with a pleasant and memorable learning experience. In this chapter, we are going to discuss the trainer's role in helping teachers (novice or experienced) understand the importance of lesson planning and offering support through the analysis, discussion and reflection that can be triggered by the exercise of putting ideas onto paper.

Catering to learners' needs

Trainers usually believe in the potential that lies within lesson planning and make good use of this in their own practice, too. It is always an interesting idea and a good exercise to think of the process of lesson planning as a metaphor. What comes to your mind? A city map? A building under construction? A forest? Scrivener (2011) compares a lesson to a "cross-country hike," and states that though the area may be unfamiliar to you, you know what to expect and bring on this journey. "What to expect" will refer to the problems you may be able to anticipate for that lesson; "what to bring" will refer to the resources and materials you plan to use, which can also be the possible solutions to your problems.

We can also get teachers to reflect upon their own perspective regarding lesson planning. This is particularly important because we can only benefit from a technique if we truly believe in it. Getting into teachers' beliefs, understanding them and provoking them are very much involved with the act of training and educating. Perhaps a good analogy would be for teachers to see a lesson plan as their road map—it includes not only their final destination (i.e., the objective of the lesson), but more importantly, how to get there (i.e., the steps and phases of the lesson). Planning the most effective lessons takes time, diligence, and an understanding of your students' goals and abilities, teaching methods and approaches, and resources.

> Planning the most effective lessons takes time, diligence, and an understanding of your students' goals and abilities...

Stating the objective of the lesson should be the starting point for the planning of any lesson—setting the objective from the beginning will better inform a teacher of the choices to be made in order to help learners achieve that objective by the end of the lesson. Apart from the main objective, a number of other core aspects for the success of a lesson should be taken into account. Below you will find a list of elements that teachers can take into consideration in their lesson planning. In order to promote more critical thinking and help teachers develop, trainers can raise teachers' awareness of these items and pose questions that will promote deeper reflection. We have also suggested some questions that you can refer to when discussing your trainees' plans:

a. Lesson aim:

i. Why have you chosen this aim?
ii. Is it a specific aim or are you focusing on something too broad?
iii. Is it measurable? Will you be able to assess whether you have achieved it by the end of the lesson?
iv. Is it something that your students are able to perform? Is it achievable, or too ambitious?
v. Can you achieve this aim within the time set for the lesson?
vi. Will you be focusing on systems or skills?
vii. Do you have any subsidiary aims?

b. The group profile:

i. Who are your students exactly?
ii. How old are they and how does their age affect their interest, involvement, attention span?
iii. How long have they been studying English?
iv. What time / day of the week is the lesson and how does that influence your students' commitment and engagement?
v. What do you know about their learning styles and learning preferences?
vi. What are their language needs?
vii. What are their affective needs?
viii. What problems can you anticipate regarding their profile and the management of the group, and how will you deal with these problems if they arise?

How much do you know about the target language that you have chosen?

c. Resources and materials:
   i. Do you need to prepare anything before the lesson?
   ii. Does the material chosen look professional?
   iii. Is the material appropriate for the profile of the group? Is it relevant?
   iv. Are there any copyright considerations that you might have overlooked?
   v. What will you have to carry with you to the classroom?
   vi. What problems can you anticipate regarding the handling of the materials or their availability and how will you deal with these problems if they arise?

d. Language analysis:
   i. What language will you expose learners to?
   ii. Do you intend to present, review, expand, contrast, or practise this language item?
   iii. How much do you know about the target language that you have chosen?
   iv. What does this language (structure or lexis) mean exactly?
   v. How is it formed?
   vi. How is it pronounced?
   vii. What problems can you anticipate regarding the meaning, form, and pronunciation of these structures (considering your specific group of students) and how will you deal with these problems if they arise?

e. Choice of activities:
   i. What kind of interaction patterns are you going to propose?
   ii. How will the activities be sequenced?
   iii. How will the instructions be given?
   iv. What is the rationale for your choice of activities?
   v. How do you plan to group students and how are they going to be sitting?
   vi. How long should each activity last?
   vii. How do you plan to move from one activity to another?
   viii. What is your role in each stage of the lesson?
   ix. How are you going to gather evidence of learning and that your aims have been achieved?

In the tasks for this chapter, we have included a possible lesson plan template that includes all of these items. When discussing the importance of lesson planning with teachers, you might want to remind them of why this exercise is so important and revisit what has to be taken into consideration when preparing a lesson. For instance, the group profile should include the number of learners in class, their age range, their strengths and weaknesses, their needs and wants. However, only listing this information does not necessarily guarantee a more effective lesson. The group's profile needs to be related, for example, to the resources and materials, which should therefore cater to these specific learners' needs, helping them achieve the lesson objective more effectively.

Enriching the learning experience

We all know that learners can be grouped in a number of different, creative ways, and the seating arrangement for the activities you propose in class can make all the difference and contribute to the success of the suggested activities. However, how often do teachers actually stop to plan this in advance, considering each group of learners and each individual learner? During the planning phase, some other questions you can ask about these aspects are the following: "Why will they be working in pairs (or in small groups)?"; "Will teenagers and adults work together or separately?"; "Will they be sitting face-to-face, back-to-back, next to each other, or in a circle?"; "How do you plan to pair learners up?".

Good classroom management is closely connected to appropriate allocation of time, clear instructions and effective monitoring. Timing, for instance, has to be well thought of beforehand so that the activities in the lesson are carried out at a brisk pace, ensuring a good level of dynamism and keeping learners on task, without rushing them. Teachers need to be able to justify, based on their knowledge of learners, why certain activities will take longer than others. Likewise, well-planned and clear instructions should contribute to learners standing a better chance of doing the proposed activities more successfully. Checking instructions before learners start doing the activity may be of great help to those learners who would not ask the teacher to repeat what they were supposed to do; a good plan should include ideas on how these instructions will be checked to ensure it is done in a confident and consistent manner.

While monitoring learners, teachers will be able not only to notice whether instructions have been clear or not, but will also be able to check if learners are on task, manage discipline, provide learners with incidental language, correct what they say and gather samples of their production for feedback on their performance. A good plan shows that teachers are aware of what they intend to do while learners are working together.

It is of paramount importance to help trainees understand the rationale underlying the phases of the lesson they are planning so that the whole picture makes sense to them. Owning their plans (and consequently their lessons) will empower novice teachers to make more informed decisions when on-the-spot changes and alterations need to be made to the plan as the lesson unfolds. Moreover, with a clearer image of their "road map" in their minds, these decisions will begin to happen in a more organic fashion as they begin to gain and draw on their experience.

All the above mentioned criteria are, first and foremost, to be taken and followed according to the institution's beliefs and views. This stage—coaching novice teachers and helping them make informed decisions to plan their lessons—will be fundamental in building not only rapport between trainer and trainee, but will also help the latter build up confidence and foster autonomy. Some language institutes may have higher expectations regarding lesson planning than others, some may have an institutionalised template, others may not refer to written notes at all. Regardless of the organisation's policy, it is of paramount importance to know what their procedures are and make sure novice teachers become acquainted with them as well, and this can go to levels outside the classroom environment, too. Richards and Farrell (2011) state, and we agree, that "becoming familiar with the physical layout of the school, its resources and resource centers ... is an important first step in preparing for a teacher practice assignment."

Developing this kind of knowledge is part of the process of lesson planning. If we think about the use of the resources and materials the school has available for teachers to plan and use in their lessons, for example, this means that teachers need to know where to find them prior to the lesson. If we consider the facilities in the school, teachers need to know whether these can be used during their lessons, if they need to be booked and, if so, how to do it and who to speak to, for instance.

Fostering autonomy and measuring learners' progress

To contribute to the process of helping trainee teachers become autonomous while planning lessons, it can be quite handy to help them become aware of the repertoire that they are creating (both in terms of approaches/activities and actual resources). Teachers can be encouraged, for example, to refer to a set of resources when thinking about their classes—which may include practical materials (such as Cuisenaire rods and Sticky Tack™) and adaptable, ready-to-use activities (such as games and warm-up tasks, among others). Cuisenaire rods (usually found for sale at educational toy shops) can be used for numberless

> After the lesson has been taught, it is vital that the teacher find the time to evaluate their plan...

activities in class, some of which include storytelling, teaching pronunciation, practising grammar (e.g., affirmative, negative and interrogative structures) and grouping students. Sticky Tack™ is also a multi-purpose resource that can, for example, hold pictures and postcards up on the walls, or display learners' production for peer feedback. The set of ready-to-use activities can be a useful solution when something does not work according to what was planned or when there are a couple of minutes to spare at the end of the lesson (which can be allocated in the plan for unexpected problems or extra practise). Once again, the activity to be used will depend on a number of factors that only the teacher of that group will be able to decide on (based on the learners' profiles, needs, etc.), and could be one of the possible solutions to the problems that were anticipated in the planning stage.

After the lesson has been taught, it is vital that the teacher find the time to evaluate their plan and how much learners have profited from the lesson. Brown (1994) states that this evaluation can be "formal or informal," which means that the teacher may or may not register this evaluation, and may or may not discuss it with a peer. Ur (1996) highlights the importance of referring to student learning in this evaluation; after all, learners are the reason why we teach in the first place. The following criteria suggested by Ur can be used to guide the reflection after the lesson has been taught and inform the steps to be followed in the light of this evaluation:

1. the class seemed to be learning the material well;
2. the learners were engaged with the foreign language throughout;
3. the learners were attentive all the time;
4. the learners enjoyed the lesson and were motivated;
5. the learners were active all the time;
6. the lesson went according to plan;
7. the language was used communicatively throughout.

Comprehensive
lesson planning will
certainly contribute to
a successful lesson.

Reflecting upon these aspects of the lesson can bring many insights and help shed some light on the reasons why some aspects of the lesson were more successful than others. This evaluation is crucial for improving not only the lesson planning stage, but also to building up teachers' repertoire of teaching techniques, which will consequently contribute to a pleasant and effective learning experience.

To wrap this chapter up, we will suggest a few tips that can be useful when planning an English lesson and that can also be added to your trainees' repertoire. You certainly have other tips to share and help us improve this list; we would love to hear them.

Plan your lesson carefully: Comprehensive lesson planning will certainly contribute to a successful lesson. Consider planning your lesson from where you want your learners to be at the end of it; in other words, start from the main objective (what you want your learners to be better able to do by the end of the lesson), and then plan how you are going to help them to get there: which text(s)—spoken or written—you are going to use as a source of language, which language items you are going to extract from there, how you are going to help them notice that language, which opportunities for contextualized practice you are going to provide them with, and how you are finally going to set the scene for them to put everything they have learned in this lesson into practice to try and achieve the objective of the lesson. And always remember that in class, it is the learners you will teach—and not the plan! (Scrivener, 2011)

Having a plan B (and sometimes a C, a D...): It is vital for a teacher to be prepared for things that may go wrong in their lessons. "Expect the unexpected," as they say. You may have found the best YouTube video to use in your lesson, or that perfect website that matches beautifully with the topic of your lesson. But if you are not prepared for a bad internet connection at the time of your lesson, and those are the only resources you have, you can be in trouble. It might seem like an exaggeration, but many colleagues have confessed to having to go out of their way to make up for lack of preparation. It is also important to bear in mind factors such as tasks not being properly graded for the level of your learners (and they may face more difficulties than you had expected—or

> ...if you're not prepared for a bad connection at the time of your lesson, and those are the only resources you have for this lesson, you can be in trouble.

the other way around); teaching a lesson on a holiday eve (when most learners are likely to be absent); a power failure; or even learners willing to focus on an unexpected event that has recently happened and which could be a perfect moment for a Dogme (Thornbury, 2006) lesson.

Teachable moments: Oftentimes teachers want so much to use all the special activities that have been prepared for that specific lesson that there is a chance they may overlook precious teachable moments which could easily turn out to be learners' most memorable experiences in the EFL classroom. A single learner-made comment, a reference to an important (or not) event, a new word learners have identified in a song or in a film—all these are examples of moments in a lesson that could serve as a springboard for a memorable learning experience. Stopping an activity to focus on a cultural aspect that could be vital for learners in an interaction with a native speaker of the language, for instance, will certainly add a spark of originality to your lesson. Johnson & Rinvolucri (2010) highlight the importance of intercultural competence in communication, and state that we need to "carry out activities to get students reflecting on culture." Taking advantage of a teachable moment certainly lends itself to help learners become more culturally aware.

Opportunities for practice and expression of creativity: After having been exposed to and having noticed new language items in class, it is important for learners to have plenty of opportunities to practise such new items with the teacher's guidance and support. These opportunities will be more effective when in a clear and meaningful context for learners, and if they are also given the chance to be creative in these tasks, adding their own contributions and making the activity much more relevant for them, learners can only win. Pugliese (2010) says that "Creativity is a key that will open many doors;" these doors can be the opportunities learners will have when interacting in English with foreigners, for instance, or that will help them get the job of their dreams. He also says that creativity is "any teacher's bread and butter." Use your own creativity to inspire learners to use theirs!

> Learners count on their teacher's guidance to let them know how they are doing in the course.

Strategies: Helping learners get better prepared for "real-life" communication is key. One of the most useful strategies to help them develop is paraphrasing (repeating something written or spoken using different words), which is done quite frequently when we visit an English-speaking country and do not know the exact word to refer to something we want or need, for example. The practice of paraphrasing can happen in an activity as simple as a vocabulary review (when in pairs, for instance, one of the learners explains a lexical item and the other says what the item is). In order to emulate a real-life situation, instructions to a speaking activity with a focus on fluency should advise learners to paraphrase items they are not sure how to say in English. By doing so, not only will they practise the strategy, but they will also keep the conversation going.

Feedback: It is only fair that learners receive feedback on their performance. Learners count on their teacher's guidance to let them know how they are doing in the course—where they are getting it right and which areas they should devote more attention to. When teachers monitor learners in an oral practice activity, they should collect samples of language for the feedback moment that can first give learners a sense of achievement and progress, and then help them develop accuracy, focusing on error correction and language expansion. Learners need such an opportunity to gauge their performance and to receive an action plan for the areas they are supposed to focus more on.

Use your own creativity to inspire learners to use theirs!

© feelplus/Shutterstock.com

References:

Brown, D. (1994) *Teaching by Principles: an Interactive Approach to Language Pedagogy.* Essex: Pearson.

Johnson, G. & Rinvolucri, M. (2010) *Culture in our Classrooms: Teaching Language Through Cultural Content.* Delta Publishing, Cengage Learning.

Pugliese, C. (2010) *Being Creative.* Surrey: Delta Publishing.

Richards, J. & Farrell, T. (2011) *Practice Teaching – A Reflective Approach.* Cambridge: CUP.

Scrivener, J. (2011) *Learning Teaching.* Oxford: Macmillan.

Thornbury, S. (2006) *An A – Z of ELT.* Oxford: Macmillan.

Ur, P. (1996) *A Course in English Language Teaching.* Cambridge: CUP.

Tasks for Chapter 3

Task 1
Giving feedback on a lesson plan

In this chapter, we discussed the importance of a carefully planned lesson and how this can impact learners' experience in the EFL classroom. It is the trainer's role to make novice teachers aware of how important it is to think of all the details in a lesson, to remind them to anticipate possible problems and think of possible solutions, and to make sure the lesson caters to their learners' needs. To make sure these and all other details described in this chapter have been catered for in a plan, it is crucial to advise trainees and novice teachers to write detailed lesson plans. By doing so, trainees will have the opportunity to think their lessons through, and trainers will be better able to provide guided help to the teachers they are assisting, pointing out strengths and weaknesses in their plans, and this will also help them develop a more holistic view of the lesson planning stage.

In this task, you will analyse a lesson plan, identify positive aspects and areas for improvement, and give feedback on the plan to a trainee teacher. The questions below should be able to help you identify the abovementioned areas, but you will also need to choose your words carefully when writing your comments – it is vital that you remember you once were an inexperienced teacher, too, and that your ideas for a lesson might not have been exactly the most conducive to learning – so consider asking questions that will help them understand your point rather than simply state they have written something wrong.

When reading your trainee's plan, make sure you have the following questions in mind:

1. **Lesson aim:** Is the aim of the lesson clear? Will it attempt to enable learners to be better able to do something with the language at the end of this lesson? Is it achievable in the time frame of the lesson? Is it relevant to this group of learners?

2. **Group profile:** Do I have enough information on this group's needs and wants? Do I know their age range? What are their predominant learning styles and affective needs?

3. **Resources and materials:** Are the resources and materials appropriate? Do they cater for the learners' needs and help them achieve the aim of the lesson? Are

they in accordance with the learners' linguistic level? Do they pose the right level of challenge?

4. **Sequencing and staging:** Does the sequence of activities make sense? Are the stages coherently linked? Are there any abrupt changes of topic from one step to another?

5. **Timing:** Is the time allotted to the activities adequate? Is it ambitious? Or is there too much time for the activities?

6. **Grouping:** Are there enough patterns of interaction in this lesson? How will learners be grouped or paired up? How will they be seated? Or will they be standing?

7. **Anticipated problems and suggested solutions:** Have problems regarding different aspects of the lesson been anticipated (e.g. technological problems, latecomers, power outage, a broken weblink in a presentation, low number of students on a holiday eve, etc)? Are the suggested solutions in the plan in accordance with the problems?

8. **Language analysis:** Does the teacher seem to have covered all aspects of the target language in the plan – meaning, use, pronunciation and form? Have anticipated problems regarding the target language been included? What about possible solutions?

9. **Learner autonomy:** Are there enough moments in the lesson for learners to work on learning strategies and for them to develop autonomy? Are these strategies relevant and adequate to this group of learners?

10. **Evidence of learning:** How will the teacher know if the lesson has been effective and if the objective has been achieved? How do they plan to collect evidence of learning? How will learners be told about their progress in this lesson?

Using the questions above as reference, analyse the lesson plan below which you have fictitiously received by email from a trainee teacher. Imagine the plan will also be sent back by email, so one idea is for you to edit the plan using the comments function on Word©. In the key, we suggest the areas and aspects we would focus on, as well as the questions we would ask the trainee teacher. These questions do not always aim at helping trainees identify mistakes in their plans, but also aim at aiding them to think more holistically when planning their lessons.

Teacher: _____

Tutor: _____

Date: _____

Lesson Number	Level of group	Number of Ss	Minutes
05	Intermediate	12	45

Lesson Aims (By the end of the lesson Ss will be better able to…)	Main aim: By the end of the lesson, students will have developed their listening skills. Sub aim: By the end of the lesson students will be more aware of the use of linking sounds as a useful sub-skill for better understanding of listening passages.

Target Language (examples of sentences and/or vocabulary)	What did you do last weekend? / Go to bed / Go shopping / Stay in / Go out / To be useless at (something) / To be rubbish at (something)

Anticipated Difficulties (task and classroom management)	1) The listening task is divided into four short dialogues and sts might not have enough time to write down their answers when doing 'listening for specific information'. 2) Some students tend to contribute more than others. 3) While doing the second part of the 'listening for specific information' phase, some sts may not be able to understand the word to be completed at all

Suggested Solutions	1) T will play and pause for a while between each conversation/dialogue. 2) T calls on Sts. 3) T will play some listening snippets more than once.

Instruction Checking (examples of how you intend to check your instructions)	Ask students to repeat/paraphrase instructions to their classmates. Ask ICQs.	**Materials and Resources**	Intermediate Outcomes Audio CD, Digital flipchart pages and handouts (see attachments for further reference).

Individual Aims (areas of teaching you wish to develop in this lesson)	I hope to carry out a student-centered lesson.

Language Analysis – Analyse the language to be presented/practised in this lesson, covering the meaning of the target structure or lexical items, an analysis of the form and specific pronunciation features. You should also anticipate difficulties that your learners might face regarding *meaning, form* and *pronunciation* and suggest how you will deal with them (*CCQs, teaching strategies, explanations, systematizations, illustrations, techniques*).

	Analysis	Anticipated difficulties	Solutions
Meaning	1) **Stay in** = to remain in your home for a period of time 2) I'm **useless** at shooting = not being able to do a certain activity 3) I'm **rubbish** at football = not being good at something 4) To **shoot** = to kick a ball 5) To **leave** (someone) = to put someone or something somewhere *Adapted from Macmillan English Dictionary Online*	3) Confusion with the noun 'rubbish'. 5) Sts might not be familiar with the past form 'left' which will appear in the listening passage.	3) CCQs: Is it a positive or negative adjective? (neg) Can the speaker play football well? (no) Is it formal or informal? (informal) 5) T boards: leave - infinitive / left - past
Form	1) **Stay in** = phrasal verb 2) To be **useless** at (something) = adjective 3) To be **rubbish** at (something) = adjective, very informal 4) To **shoot** = verb 5) To **leave** = verb	*As these expressions will be dealt in receptive skills, 'form' might not be a major problem.*	
Pronunciation	1) **Stay in** /steɪ ɪn/ 2) I'm **useless** at … /aɪmˈjuːslɪs/ * *the sound is linked 3) To be rubbish at … /ˈrʌbɪʃ/ 4) To **shoot** = verb /ʃuːt/ 5) To **leave** = verb /liːv/	2) *Sts might pronounce /u/ instead of /uː/* 3) *Sts might pronounce /u/ instead of /ʌ/ /r/ sound at the beginning of the word?* 5) *Sts might pronounce the /i/ instead of /iː/*	Drill + board phonemic symbols when necessary.

Stage	Stage Aim	Time	Inter action	Procedure	Comments
Lead-in	To engage students to the topic (weekend activities);	14'	T-sts Sts-sts T-sts	Material: Flipchart pages 1, 2 and 3. • T asks what day of the week is today in order to quickly revise the days of the week and the meaning of 'weekend'. • T asks what sts usually do at the weekend and also clarifies the meaning of 'stay in' and 'go out'. T boards sts' contribution. • T pairs up sts to discuss the question 'What do you like doing at the weekend'? • T provides sts with constructive feedback.	
Set the scene	To engage students for the next phase and activate their schemata.	3'	T-sts	• T asks if they remember what they did last weekend and if they liked it or not? T also asks if they felt 'enthusiastic' about their weekend in order to get sts better prepared to understand the question in the next phase.	
Listening for gist	To check/ develop sts' understanding of the overall tone of the message.	5'	Indiv. T-sts	Material: Flipchart p.4 + Audio CD tracks 4.1, 4.2, 4.3, 4.4 • T shows the question on the board and check sts' understanding (question on page 4). "How many conversations are we going to listen to?" (four) "How many conversations are we going to choose?" (one) "Are we going to choose a conversation in which the speaker shows more or less enthusiasm?" (more) • T corrects with the whole group and elicits evidence.	
Listening for specific information (1)	To check/ develop sts' understanding of specific information in the text.	9'	Indiv.	Material: flipchart p.4 + handout • T tells sts they are going to listen to the dialogues again, and ask them to write down 'what the speakers did and when'. T plays and pauses between each conversation. • T corrects with the whole group and boards answers.	
Listening for specific information (2)	To check sts' understanding of some more detailed information as well as call their attention to linking sounds.	5'	Indiv.	Material: flipchart p.5 + handout • T plays the fourth conversation again and asks sts to fill in the gaps. Most of the words that sts should write down are content words (local, useless etc). Some of the words are not, such as 'then' and 'but', and were removed from the text in order to call sts' attention to linking sounds, which will be later dealt in the next phase.	

Follow-up (1)	To make students aware of linking sounds.	2'	Sts-sts	Material: flipchart p.6 • T helps sts notice the linking sound in the first sentence and (if time allows) asks them to decide in pairs where the linking sounds should be placed in the other sentences. • T collects sts' contribution. Drill.
Follow-up (2) *(If time allows)*	To provide sts with an extended practice of the listening topic.	5'	Sts-sts	Material: flipchart p.7 • In pairs sts ask each other 'what did you do (last weekend)?'
Feedback	To raise sts' awareness of areas to be improved and good performances as well as to give them the opportunity to share their conversations.	2'	T-Sts	• T asks some students to report what they have talked, and occasionally writes down some examples of good and bad production, and wraps-up the lesson.

Key – (Suggested points to be addressed by tutor (highlighted), as well as suggested comments to be made (in orange).)

Lesson Aims *(By the end of the lesson Ss will be better able to…)*	**Main aim:** By the end of the lesson, students will have developed their <u>listening skills</u>. (Tutor: Could you be more specific? Is your focus on listening for gist or specific information, for example?) **Sub aim:** By the end of the lesson students will be more aware of the use of linking sounds as a useful sub-skill for better understanding listening passages.

Target Language *(examples of sentences and/or vocabulary)*	What did you do last weekend? / Go to bed / Go shopping / Stay in / Go out / To be useless at (something) / To be rubbish at (something)

Anticipated Difficulties *(task and classroom management)*	1) The listening task is divided into four short dialogues and sts might not have enough time to write down their answers when doing 'listening for specific information'. 2) Some students tend to contribute more than others. 3) While doing the second part of the 'listening for specific information' phase, some sts may not be able to understand the word to be completed at all (Tutor: Is it possible to adapt this?)

Suggested Solutions *(task and classroom management)*	1) T will play and pause for a while between each conversation/dialogue. (Tutor: Good idea!) 2) T nominates Sts. (Tutor: For cohesion here, use "will nominate".) 3) T will play some listening snippets **for** more than once. (Tutor: No preposition needed here.)

Instruction Checking *(examples of how you intend to check your instructions)*	Ask students to repeat/paraphrase instructions to their classmates. Ask ICQs. (Tutor: Good. Also, make sure you plan your ICQs beforehand (you may even have them written down in your plan).)	**Materials and Resources**	Intermediate Outcomes Audio CD, Digital flipchart pages and handouts (see attachments for further reference).

Individual Aims *(areas of teaching you wish to develop in this lesson)*	I hope to carry out a student-centered lesson. (Tutor: This is a good individual aim. What do you plan to do to achieve it?)

Language Analysis – Analyse the language to be presented/practised in this lesson, covering the meaning of the target structure or lexical items, an analysis of the form and specific pronunciation features. You should also anticipate difficulties that your learners might face regarding *meaning, form and pronunciation* and suggest how you will deal with them (*CCQs, teaching strategies, explanations, systematizations, illustrations, techniques*).

	Analysis	Anticipated difficulties	Solutions
Meaning	1) Stay in = to remain in your home for a period of time 2) I'm useless at shooting = not being able to do a certain activity 3) I'm rubbish at football = not being good at something 4) To shoot = to kick a ball 5) To leave (someone) = to put someone or something somewhere *Adapted from Macmillan English Dictionary Online*	3) Confusion with the noun 'rubbish'. 5) Sts might not be familiar with the past form 'left' which will appear in the listening passage.	3) CCQs: (Tutor: Good CCQs. Consider writing some for the other terms as well.) Is it a positive or negative adjective? (neg) Can the speaker play football well? (no) Is it formal or informal? (informal) 5) T boards: leave - infinitive / left - past
Form	1) Stay in = phrasal verb 2) To be useless at (something) = adjective 3) To be rubbish at (something) = adjective, very informal 4) To shoot = verb 5) To leave = verb	As these expressions will be dealt in receptive skills, 'form' might not be a major problem. (Tutor: What if they prevent meaning from being understood? How will you deal with that?)	
Pronunciation	1) Stay in /steɪ_ɪn/ (Tutor: There's a linking /j/ here, too.) 2) I'm useless at ... /aɪm'juːslɪs/ *the sound is linked 3) To be rubbish at ... /'rʌbɪʃ/ 4) To shoot = verb /ʃuːt/ 5) To leave = verb /liːv/	2) Sts might pronounce /u/ instead of /uː/ 3) Sts might pronounce /u/ instead of /ʌ/ (Tutor: What about the /r/ sound at the beginning of the word? Isn't it more likely to be mispronounced by learners?) 5) Sts might pronounce the /i/ instead of /iː/	Drill + board phonemic symbols when necessary.

Stage	Stage Aim	Time	Inter action	Procedure	Comments
Lead-in	To engage students <u>to</u> the topic (weekend activities); (Tutor: in)	<u>14'</u> (Tutor: Could this stage be shorter?)	T-sts Sts-sts T-sts	Material:- Flipchart pages 1, 2 and 3. • T asks what day of the week <u>is today</u> in order to quickly revise the days of the week and the meaning of 'weekend'. (Tutor: careful with language – use an embedded question here.) • T asks what sts usually do at the weekend and also clarifies the meaning of 'stay in' and 'go out'. T boards sts' contribution. • T pairs up sts to discuss the question 'What do you like doing at the weekend'? • T provides sts with <u>constructive feedback</u>. (Tutor: Good to focus on positive aspects here.)	
<mark>Set the scene</mark> (Tutor: For cohesion, use an –ing form here.)	To engage students for the next phase and activate their schemata.	3'	T-sts	• T asks if they remember what they did last weekend and if they liked it or <u>not?</u> (Tutor: Punctuation (a period should be used here)), T also asks if they felt 'enthusiastic' about their weekend in order to get sts better prepared to understand the question in the next phase.	
Listening for gist	To check/ develop sts' understanding of the overall tone of the message.	5'	Indiv. T-sts	Material:- Flipchart p.4 + Audio CD tracks 4.1, 4.2, 4.3, 4.4 • T shows the question on the board and <u>check</u> sts' understanding (question on page 4). (Tutor: SV agreement – check<u>s</u>) "How many conversations are we going to listen to?" (four) "How many conversations are we going to choose?" (one) "Are we going to choose a conversation in which the speaker shows more or less enthusiasm?' (more) • T corrects with the whole group and elicits evidence.	
Listening for specific information (1)	To check/ develop sts' understanding of specific information in the text.	9'	Indiv.	Material:- flipchart p.4 + handout • T tells sts they are going to listen to the dialogues again, and <u>ask</u> (Tutor: SV agreement - ask<u>s</u>) them to write down 'what the speakers did and when'. T plays and pauses between each conversation. • <u>T corrects with the whole group and boards answers</u>. (Tutor: Good to help visual learners and for Ss to check their answers, too.)	

Listening for specific information (2)	To check sts' understanding of some more detailed information as well as call their attention to linking sounds.	5'	Indiv.	Material: flipchart p.5 + handout • T plays the fourth conversation again and asks sts to fill in the gaps. Most of the words that sts should write down are content words (local, useless etc). Some of the words are not, such as 'then' and 'but', and were removed from the text in order to <u>call</u> sts' attention to linking sounds (Tutor: draw), which will be <u>later dealt</u> in the next phase. (Tutor: dealt with later)
Follow-up (1)	To make students aware of linking sounds.	<u>2'</u> (Tutor: Are 2' enough for this?)	Sts-sts	Material: flipchart p.6 • T helps sts notice the linking sound in the first sentence and (if time allows) asks them to decide in pairs where the linking sounds should be placed in the other sentences. • T collects sts' contribution. <u>Drill.</u> (Tutor: for coherence, use "T drills")
Follow-up (2) – (If time allows) (Tutor: Good to have a flexi-stage.)	To provide sts with an extended practice of the listening topic.	5'	Sts-Sts	Material: flipchart p.7 • In pairs sts ask each other 'what did you do (last weekend)?'
Feedback (Tutor: This stage is truly important, and you may consider allotting more time to it here.)	To raise sts' awareness of areas to be improved and good performances as well as to give them the opportunity to share their conversations.	2' (Tutor: Again, are 2' enough?)	T-Sts	• Tasks some students to report what they have <u>talked</u> (Tutor: discussed), and <u>occasionally</u> (Tutor: Funny choice of word here...) writes down some examples of good and bad production, and wraps-up the lesson.

Chapter 4

Observing lessons

"Lesson observations may trigger the most diverse reactions, be it the first time or the fiftieth time this happens. While some will dread having an observer in their classroom, and may even face stage fright, others might enjoy the experience and even invite peers or supervisors to come into their classroom."

Lesson observations may trigger the most diverse reactions, be it the first time or the fiftieth time this happens. While some will dread having an observer in their classroom, and may even face stage fright, others might enjoy the experience and even invite peers or supervisors to come into their classroom. Observing a trainee teacher in action is a logical and natural follow-up procedure to help teachers develop professionally because it might provide very helpful insights as to what really goes on in the lesson. After all, as Richards and Lockhart (1996) say, "much of what happens in teaching is unknown to the teacher." It is therefore a privilege to sit in quietly and simply witness all the interactions and dynamics of a lesson in order to help teachers become more aware of what is actually taking place. However, some trainers still choose to refrain from observing teachers more often because of the discomfort that might be generated. So, in order to avoid a potential negative feeling, lesson observations (as a tool for professional development) might be neglected or underused. Hence, we truly believe that it is very important to demystify lesson observations so as to associate them with a more positive experience and promote a more conscious and consistent exploitation of such a rich developmental resource.

There is a simple story about a girl and a pianist that we find particularly illustrative of how a more experienced professional can contribute to someone who does not have the same experience by closely observing what they do. The story is the following:

> *A mother, who wished to encourage her small girl's interest in the piano, took her to a local concert featuring an excellent pianist but got distracted and lost her daughter in the entrance foyer. With the concert due to start, the girl had still not been found. The curtains drew aside, to reveal the little girl sitting at the great piano, focused in concentration, quietly picking out the notes of "Twinkle, Twinkle, Little Star." The audience's amusement turned to curiosity when the pianist entered the stage, walked up to the little girl, and said, "Keep playing." The pianist sat down beside her, listened for a few seconds, and whispered some more words of encouragement. He then began quietly to play a bass accompaniment. At the end of the impromptu performance the audience applauded loudly as the pianist took the little girl back to her seat to be reunited with her mother.*

> Teacher educators should try to act as mentors of the novice teachers in all the contexts of the profession...

The generosity of the pianist and the trust and boldness of the girl are inspiring. As teacher educators, we cannot help but associate the interaction above with overall professional development, and especially with classroom observation. Ideally, as educators, we should welcome the opportunity to be guided and helped so that we can get better results – and, working within the analogy, get a standing ovation from our students. Teacher educators should try to act as mentors of the novice teachers in all the contexts of the profession (including during the actual lesson); and a mentoring relationship is based on a positive connection as described by Bailey *et al.* (2001), "Mentoring is an interpersonal, ongoing, situated, supportive, and informative professional relationship between two (or more) individuals, one of whom (the mentor) has more experience in the profession, craft, or skill in question." So, why is it that classroom observation usually generates so much uneasiness as opposed to its original idea of being a means to a positive and supportive experience that aims at improving teaching?

We sympathise with the anxiety that teachers often feel when being observed and understand the challenges of having a new element in your safe environment—someone who is taking notes on everything you do. For this reason, we would like to suggest certain principles that can help trainers show teachers how they can benefit a bit more from what some may describe as a "painful" experience.

State the purpose clearly – There are several institutional reasons why a teacher is observed. Unless professionals are convinced that the objective is to work together in order to reflect upon practice and develop, imagination is likely to take a much less inspiring route. The fear of being assessed, judged, or criticised can certainly interfere with the outcome. And the true and positive intention might be misunderstood, creating unnecessary stress. It is therefore vital that teachers be told in advance why you are going to observe them. Transparency is key.

Discuss the plan – An observer could certainly drop by unannouncedly. However, if the objective is professional development, it might be more reassuring to give the observed teacher the best possible chance to succeed. It is really important to encourage the teacher to write a clear and thorough

> Classroom observation should generate an interesting and accurate feedback session.

lesson plan to be discussed before the actual observation. This pre-meeting will give the observed teacher an opportunity to rethink their decisions and set a clearer scene as to what they are aiming at. Other important information might come up in this discussion as well, such as details about the group, the students' needs, and possible difficulties with the material or the content, not to mention that it will naturally strengthen the bond with the observer and hopefully open a channel for further consulting.

Get a copy of the plan – Although the plan will have been discussed, it is easier for the observer to follow the teacher's ideas if they keep a copy of the plan. Even if the plan is changed during the class, these on-the-spot decisions can be better understood and discussed if the observer has the original rationale in their hands. The observer will be able to point out aspects related to the sequence of activities, timing, and interaction patterns, for instance.

Inform the group – Having an observer in the classroom is often just as uncomfortable for the students. That is why it is really important for the observer to keep a relaxed atmosphere, interacting with the students before and after the class. Being professional and serious is often mistaken for being unfriendly. An observer should be a role model. And how can they discuss good rapport if they sit down, open their notebooks, and leave without acknowledging the existence of the students? Another concern is that teachers sometimes wonder how to explain to the students the presence of a stranger. Saying that it is simply the school's policy to encourage observation of lessons sounds reasonable and true and may help the teacher feel a little less in the spotlight. Another important aspect to take into account is where you are going to sit during the observation. You may want to ask the teacher to save a place for you by the door, especially if you should leave the lesson before it finishes (or enter after it has started) so that no greater commotion is caused by your entering/leaving the classroom.

Keep track of instances – Classroom observation should generate an interesting and accurate feedback session. So it is really important to keep track of valid instances of what the students and the teacher actually said, what was written on the board, or how

> One can certainly observe different aspects of a teacher's class (use of language, classroom management, giving instructions, monitoring, methodology, etc.)

the students reacted. Using the names of the students in the report helps the teacher remember the exact moment when something happened. For instance, the observer needs to make an effort to focus on the facts and describe the lesson in concrete ways, so that judgment, rushed conclusions, or personal opinions do not prevail.

Focus – One can certainly observe different aspects of a teacher's class (use of language, classroom management, giving instructions, monitoring, methodology, etc.). And that often happens in the first observation, when the observer has their first contact with that teacher's style. However, it might help to come back to the second observation with a couple of priorities in mind. This way, both the observer and the observed teacher can pay closer attention to more specific features of their teaching. It is also relevant to invite the observed teacher to choose what they want the observer to focus on. Allowing the teacher to participate more actively in the observation process will give them a greater sense of responsibility and the motivation to feel heard and valued.

Create a code – Most institutions have their own form to be used during the observation. Other observers write their notes on the actual lesson plan. Whatever document is used, it is always a good idea to create some general codes to help organise the notes during the class. A check for what was successful, a star for when an aim is achieved, a dot for something that didn't work very well are some examples of small things that can save quite a lot of time and help the reading of the report. It is important to remember that as challenging as it may seem, the report needs to be written at a fast pace (during the lesson) but not at the expense of a clear organisation of ideas. Therefore, planning what the report is going to look like and how it is going to be structured might help trainers with a more effective communication of what they observe.

Give feedback – Being patted on the back and getting a "Very Good" cannot be considered feedback. This is one of the most important parts of this process and needs to take place as soon as possible after the class, while things are still fresh in both the observer's and the teacher's minds. A good amount of time needs to be set for this to be done calmly and with no interruptions.

Be coherent and transparent – Asking questions and encouraging the teacher to come up with their own answers is an excellent exercise to encourage reflection. However, teachers often say that they crave clearer feedback as to what was good and what could be improved. We believe that it is important to keep a balance between telling, asking, and guiding. It is very important to say when there was something excellent, too! Words of encouragement must always come in a genuine way. This often seems to be forgotten and then feedback may lack coherent praising.

Prioritise – If the observer chooses to analyse several aspects of teaching and delve into each and every stage of the lesson, there has got to be a set of priorities in the end. Three is a mystical number and it seems to fit this purpose well. Three strengths and three areas to be improved can summarise the observation and give the teacher something to focus on, as a plan of action for further development. However, merely pointing these features out will not be enough, unless the teacher is helped to analyse how they can improve and what exactly needs to be done.

Share the report – During feedback, lots of points will be discussed and hopefully new ideas will arise, too. The teachers will need time to let things sink in. Giving a copy of the report for them to refer to is a strategy that observers can use to encourage continuous reflection. It also allows the teacher to participate more actively during the feedback session since they know they will get the report and do not need to write everything down.

Follow up – Observations will be more effective if they happen on a regular basis. The observer must give the teachers time to experiment and digest all that was discussed before coming back. When the second or third observation is set, a careful analysis of the strengths and areas to be developed from the previous observation(s) will help the observer evaluate how the teacher has progressed.

The importance of observing lessons and acting upon the stages related to the teaching (pre and post lesson observation) is acknowledged by many. Woodward (1992), for example, says that "a major part of most trainers' work is helping trainees to plan, prepare and observe lessons and watch trainees teach." Thus, we think it is high time we demystified classroom observation and started looking at it from a much more positive perspective. Observers should follow the same principles they expect their trainees to follow regarding rapport, feedback, affective needs and encouragement. After all, we are all working together for the excellence of teaching. It is true that one does not learn a language the same way one learns how to play the piano. But a teacher trainer (or observer) might be compared to the pianist who, so willingly and generously, believed in and guided someone who wanted to improve. Teacher educators have the responsibility, as more senior professionals, to work towards a new perspective regarding lesson observations; and having a positive attitude regarding all the variables involved in observing teachers is of paramount importance. After all, it takes just a few moments to make somebody's day, to help someone with their own personal aims and dreams— especially someone who looks up to you for encouragement and support.

References:

Bailey, K., Curtis, A. and Nunan, D. (2001) *Pursuing Professional Development: Self as Source*. Boston: Heinle and Heinle.

Richards, J. and Lockhart, C. (1996) *Reflective Teaching in Second Language Classrooms*. New York: Cambridge University Press.

Woodward, T. (1992) *Ways of Training*. Harlow: Longman.

Tasks for Chapter 4

In this chapter, we discussed the importance of a lesson observation, as well as how teachers usually feel about it and the impacts an observation can have on a lesson and on the performance of a teacher. We also discussed the many advantages a lesson observation can have on a teacher's professional development, and how the support given to a trainee teacher before and after the observation can also be of great value.

An important factor to always bear in mind when observing a lesson is that there should always be a clear focus for the observation. A trainee teacher might have a number of areas to develop, but pointing them out all at once after the first observation can be quite overwhelming, thus the importance of focusing on some specific points (rather than on all of them) at a time. In figure 1 (see on page 65) we suggest a form to be used by the trainer when observing novice teachers bearing this important aspect in mind.

Since many teachers might feel rather uncomfortable with the observation of a supervisor, we would like to propose some alternative types of observation in order to lower the trainees' anxiety and help them get more used to the process itself, highlighting the many benefits an extra pair of eyes (and ears) can have on a teacher's performance inside the classroom.

The three types of observation we would like to propose here have different objectives and outcomes as well. The suggestions are the following: (1) audio or video record a lesson; (2) peer observations; and (3) "blind" observations. The rationale underlying each of the suggestions, as well as their benefits and drawbacks, are listed below. We also suggest guided questions for each suggested type of observation.

1. Audio or video recording a lesson

Audio or video recording a lesson can be a way of diminishing the anxiety of having an observer in the classroom, and this practice can be a good awareness-raising activity for novice and more experienced teachers alike. If a teacher chooses to record only the audio of their lesson, it can be a great opportunity for them to focus on their classroom language, TTT (teacher talking time), or even mannerisms or language vices. If the choice is for a videoed lesson, a peer may be invited to film the delivery. If learners appear in the recording, they should be asked to sign a document giving the teacher and institution permission to use the footage (especially if learners are under age). Some questions that might help promote reflection are the following:

> a. Were my instructions clear and objective?
> b. Was there a fair balance between TTT and STT (student talking time)?
> c. Was my language appropriate for the level I was teaching?
> d. Was I a good linguistic model for my learners?
> e. Did I genuinely respond to learners' contributions?

Some possible drawbacks of this type of observation include the teacher missing out on important areas to improve in their lesson due to lack of awareness; learners being too concerned with the equipment in class and not performing like they usually do, thus impacting on the result of the lesson; and the quality of the recording not being good enough to be analysed (e.g., the sound might be too low).

2. Peer observation

Inviting a peer to observe your lesson can be of benefit to both parties, in the sense that the peer observing can broaden their teaching repertoire by learning new techniques for their practice. Moreover, teachers may feel there is less pressure on them if the observer is a peer—someone with whom they might be more used to sharing their concerns.

When inviting a peer to observe a lesson, the teacher inviting them should state beforehand what they would like the peer to focus on (e.g., giving instructions, rapport, timing, etc.). In this way, it will be easier for the observer to share their views at the end of the observation. The following questions might help set a clear focus for the observation:

> a. Do I have any blind spots (i.e., Do I unintentionally neglect any of my learners?)?
> b. How effective were my instructions? (This can be noticed by focusing on learners' reactions).
> c. Did I call on all my learners throughout the lesson?
> d. Was my board clearly organised (i.e., Could Ss easily find information there?)?

In "blind" lesson observations, supervisor and trainee plan and discuss the lesson together, but there is no lesson observation *per se*.

It is also very important that both teachers agree on the post-lesson procedures, as there might be some resentment if the observer decides to give their peer feedback on their delivery without them having asked for it. Another drawback we can anticipate here is the observer being as inexperienced as the observed teacher—how much will they be able to notice if both are still at the early stages of development?

3. "Blind" lesson observations

In "blind" lesson observations, supervisor and trainee plan and discuss the lesson together, but there is no lesson observation *per se*. However, there is a feedback session which is carried out based on the teacher's perceptions and analysis of the delivery of the lesson. Throughout the lesson, the teacher may need to take a few notes on the outcomes of the activities so that this data can inform the feedback session. It can also be a good idea for the teacher to make notes or write down their reflections in a journal, which could also be referred to during feedback. With that data in mind, tutor and teacher discuss the lesson, and they agree on a plan of action for development. If the teacher does not make a conscious effort throughout the lesson to observe all aspects that need to be observed, they may miss out on important data for the feedback session. There will be a lot of cognitive and metacognitive processing going on (e.g., following the steps of the lesson, reacting to learners' needs, adapting procedures, and taking notes of what happens in the lesson), and this can be seen as one of the major drawbacks of this type of observation.

The following set of questions might aid a teacher who decides to carry out a "blind" lesson observation:

> a. How accurate was my timing for the activities in this lesson? How much did I need to adapt?
> b. In which activities did I need to depart from the plan and react to learners' needs?
> c. How did I deal with incidental language in this lesson?
> d. Could I have used learners' contributions more genuinely in this lesson?

Figure 1 – a lesson observation form

Teacher's name:	Date:
Tutor's name:	Number of Ss in class:
Focus of the observation: (error correction)	

🕐	What the teacher did	What Ss did

- Questions for reflection before feedback session:
  (e.g., Why did you decide to do on-the-spot correction during the second practice?)

- Action plan (to be devised with tutor at the end of feedback session):
  (e.g., Do two peer observations focusing on error correction.)

How easy was it for you
to focus on the lesson
and take notes of relevant
information?

Task 1
Observing an inexperienced teacher

Use the lesson observation form above to observe an inexperienced teacher (N.B.: You may find it easier to use a laptop computer to fill out the form when you observe the lesson). When you have finished the report, revise and proofread it carefully in order to check you have not used any inadequate terms, and to spot any possible typos you may have made.

You may want to reflect upon the following questions as well:

1. How easy was it for you to focus on the lesson and take notes of relevant information?
2. How easy was it for you to list facts as opposed to stating your opinion of the activities and procedures in the lesson?
3. Were any sections of the reports more challenging than others to be filled out?
4. Would you adapt any of the sections?
5. How useful was the report in the feedback session?

> Invite a more experienced teacher in your school to try the "blind" observation technique with you.

Task 2
Filming your lesson and discussing it with a peer

Choose one of the groups you are currently teaching and use a video camera or a mobile device to record your own lesson. Invite a peer to observe the lesson with you, stating two or three areas for them to focus on while you both watch the video together. Make sure you provide your peer with a brief group profile, the objective of your lesson, and any other relevant details you think may enrich the discussion. In order to focus on details and gather as much evidence as needed, you may pause the video as many times as necessary. One of the possible follow-ups for this task would be for you to list alternative procedures should there be any activities that did not go according to plan.

Task 3
Trying out a "blind" lesson observation

Invite a more experienced teacher in your school to try the "blind" observation technique with you. Make sure you explain to them the rationale underlying this type of observation and what your objective with this procedure is. Ask them to provide you with a group profile, and make yourself available to plan the lesson together with them. After they have taught the lesson, suggest they make some notes on its strengths and weaknesses, and then get together to discuss it. You may want to focus the reflection on learners' outcomes in an attempt to help the teacher to remember details of the lesson (i.e., by helping them to focus on what learners managed to produce, it might be easier for them to reflect upon the types of activities suggested, the level of challenge posed, and the instructions given to learners). To wrap up the feedback session, the two of you may want to work on an action plan with a focus on developing your peer's teaching practice.

Chapter 5

Giving feedback

"A teacher educator will devise training sessions, help teachers plan their lessons, assist teachers with their practice by promoting moments of reflection, observe lessons, and certainly provide feedback. Feedback is an intrinsic part of the role of any teacher trainer or teacher educator; it happens on more formal and less formal occasions, and it might have the power to boost one's confidence or literally make someone give up on their career."

A teacher educator will devise training sessions, help teachers plan their lessons, assist teachers with their practice by promoting moments of reflection, observe lessons, and certainly provide feedback. Feedback is an intrinsic part of the role of any teacher trainer or teacher educator; it happens on more formal and less formal occasions, and it might have the power to boost one's confidence or literally make someone give up on their career. We believe that effective feedback from teacher educators should reflect the features identified by Freeman (1989) as a springboard for the development of their trainees: know your subject matter, use your skills as a teacher, know what you are trying to accomplish, learn to recognize results, and allow yourself to be a beginner. However challenging it may be, any feedback moment needs to display solid understanding of the teaching and learning of a foreign language, confident use of skills that are expected from a teacher, clear goals, acknowledgement of what has been achieved, and the modesty to behave as a beginner.

Considering the principles above, we would like to suggest feedback moments be carefully planned. Nonetheless, just like any effective lesson, an effective plan should not be perceived as a straitjacket but rather as guidelines that will lead you to a clear objective. It is extremely important to adapt the feedback moments according to issues, reactions, doubts, insights, resistance, or hesitations that might arise. Due to its complexity, we consider it particularly interesting to resort to andragogy and experiential learning, consider the relevance throughout the process, and instill the use of probing questions to trigger reflection in any feedback moment (whether it is a face-to-face discussion after a lesson observation, or an informal meeting to discuss career opportunities or perceptions about students). In order to maximise the learning of adults (and teachers are adults), for example, an andragogical approach can be implemented so as to involve them more naturally and expedite their growth. In andragogy, "the richest resource for learning resides in adults themselves; therefore, tapping into their experiences through experiential techniques (discussions, simulations, problem-solving activities, or case methods) is beneficial" (Knowles *et al.*, 2005, p 65). In other words, feedback might be more effective if the teacher's background is considered and validated, and if learning revolves around the actual experience, rather than a top-down lecture on what should be done.

Another strategy that we have mentioned is the use of probing questions. Probing questions seem to represent a very effective teacher development tool. They are often used to provoke deeper reflection, address the most appropriate points, guide

> ...genuine probing questions are harder to create and are often mistaken for a suggestion or a simple question that intends to clarify the matter.

teachers' perceptions, encourage autonomous thinking, and assess reactions and understanding. Wallace & Gravells (2007) say that probing questions are used extensively in exploration because "they ensure that the relevant issues have been fully examined and assumptions have not been taken for granted." It might be relevant to reinforce the difference between clarifying questions and probing questions before we move on.

According to the National School Reform Faculty (2002), clarifying questions are simple questions of fact. They clarify the dilemma and provide the nuts and bolts so that good probing questions can be asked. They have brief, factual answers, and do not provide any new "food for thought." Probing Questions, on the other hand, are intended to encourage thinking more deeply about the issue at hand. If a probing question does not have that effect, it is either a clarifying question or a recommendation. The teacher should not have a ready answer to a genuine probing question. So, whenever giving feedback, teacher educators can resort to both clarifying and probing questions. But based on our experience, genuine probing questions are harder to create and are often mistaken for a suggestion or a simple question that intends to clarify the matter. Some possible stems for probing questions (that can be used during feedback after a lesson observation or in a coaching session) are:

- Why do you think this is the case?
- What would you have to change in order to...?
- What's another way you might...?
- What would it look like if...?
- What do you think would happen if...?
- What sort of an impact do you think...?
- What criteria did you use to...?
- How did you decide/determine/conclude...?
- What was your intention when ...?
- How do you think your ... has influenced your choices?
- What did the students think/do/say? Why do you think they did it?

Giving feedback should be a consistent part of any teacher development programme and, because of its importance, should reflect the same basic principles identified by Bax (1997) when discussing larger teacher education programmes. According to him, these should be (a) appropriate, (b) context-sensitive, and (c) likely to encourage reflection and long-term change—just like any feedback. Appropriate in the sense that the boundaries of your goals as a teacher educator should respect the teachers' needs and your role in the process; context sensitive to the extent that all variables need to be taken into account, such as the teacher's experience and qualifications, their attitude towards feedback, the institutional objectives, etc.; and feedback should likewise focus on a long-term reflection that will eventually promote actual change. The challenge lies in finding the appropriate depth and selecting the most relevant features to cover. You do not want feedback to be perceived as shallow; neither do you want to over-emphasize the challenges and the areas for improvement, causing teachers to lose confidence and motivation. Balance is therefore both hard to strike and essential to find.

William (2011) makes a rather interesting statement about teachers' self-perception:

> "The only teachers who think they are successful are those who have low expectations of their students. They are the sort of teachers who say, 'What can you expect from these kids?' The answer is, of course, a lot more than the students are achieving with those teachers. The best teachers fail all the time because they have such high aspirations for what their students can achieve—generally much higher than the students themselves have."

How can feedback, for example, help teachers realise that their belief in students might be affecting the effectiveness of what they do? How can feedback help those teachers who believe they are failing to notice that this very same feeling is what makes them so good? Feedback needs to bring teachers' beliefs into the spotlight, addressing deep—oftentimes unknown—assumptions about the teaching, the learning, the students, the language, and the teachers' role. Feedback needs to help teachers look at the macro picture and stretch their understanding of their role, the students themselves, and the learning process.

In general terms, we believe that feedback should get teachers to become more critical, more aware, and more autonomous. There seems to be a lot of debate over a unified definition for critical thinking, but most researchers and teachers agree with its importance in any learning process. Brown (2004), for instance, states that in an ideal academic English program, "the objectives of a curriculum are not limited to linguistic factors alone, but also include developing the art of critical thinking." Many books and articles offer practical ideas to English teachers and encourage us to consider techniques and approaches that will help learners develop problem-solving and decision-making skills, for example. However, we feel that many language teachers feel unprepared to effectively instill critical thinking and adapt their practice so as to add a new focus on skills that go beyond the language itself. We also think that it is through feedback that teacher trainers might take advantage of what teachers already know in order to revisit initiatives that aim at professional development.

In order to reflect upon the connection between critical thinking and feedback, we would like to refer to Brookfield's (1987) definition. Brookfield states that when we think critically about a given topic, we are forced to consider our own relationship to it and how we personally fit into the context of the issue. In that sense, whenever there is an opportunity for formal or informal feedback, teacher trainers need to think of how they can help novice—and more experienced teachers—critically reflect upon their relationship to the act of teaching and learning of a foreign language, and also reflect upon the role they play in the entire process. Trainers need to provoke teachers into considering skills, knowledge, awareness, and attitudes that go beyond concrete classroom practice. It is very important that in feedback moments trainers get practitioners to look into their stance towards the students and the institution, for example, and engage in discussions that cover beliefs regarding learning, teaching, and professionalism.

If we appeal to Ennis (2003), we might be better able to outline some characteristics that a teacher educator might want to develop in the teachers they are working with via feedback. Ennis identified a number of features that are common to critical thinkers. The characteristics include: attempting to be well-informed; being open-minded and mindful of alternatives; able to judge well the credibility of sources; able to identify conclusions, reasons and assumptions; and able to judge well the quality of an argument, including its reasons, assumptions, and evidence. He also suggested that critical thinkers would most likely be able to develop and defend a reasonable position, ask clarifying questions, formulate plausible hypotheses, plan experiments well, define terms in a way appropriate for the context, and draw conclusions when warranted. If we look at the competencies that a critical thinker has, we can easily identify a number of characteristics that are also expected to be found in effective teachers.

Nevertheless, a lot of training initiatives and feedback tend to focus on a very pragmatic aspect of teaching, revolving around the implementation of mechanical techniques and the reproduction of procedures for determined tasks. Therefore, we would like to reinforce the importance of a broader scope for teacher educators' feedback that should comprise more than prescriptive tips for classroom management or automatised recipes for drilling. Feedback needs to go beyond ideas for a more engaging warm-up or the identification of classroom techniques that were "effective."

In our opinion, feedback moments are the best time to carefully consider ways to make teachers more critical thinkers. Only after teachers have become more critical themselves will they be able to change their own practice and move on to help learners develop these skills, too. Going back to the characteristics highlighted by Ennis, these are some ideas of what trainers can do in order to incorporate elements of critical thinking into their feedback:

- Assess whether teachers are really considering alternatives that go beyond their well-known repertoire of teaching and encourage conscious experimentation with varied methods, approaches, and techniques.
- Ask teachers to seek further formal knowledge (before and after feedback sessions), setting goals for research and reading—always asking for theoretical justifications for the decisions made.
- Only accept justifications that have sound theoretical background and reject sources whose credibility can be challenged, demanding reference to serious and reliable academic literature.
- Ask for the rationale behind decisions and assumptions about students, their needs, and the selected tasks—always challenging trainees to call upon their own knowledge and experience.
- Allow teachers to maintain well-informed discussions about the reasons behind their plans and the on-the-spot decisions made during their teaching.
- Raise awareness of the role that teachers play inside and outside the classroom, considering their interactions with students, fellow teachers, supervisors, and the community.
- Instill the need for continuous development and more formal studies.

Both King (1995) and Taba (1966) argue that the level of students' thinking is strongly influenced by the level of questions which are asked in class. If we take this data into the realms of teacher training and feedback, we can therefore say that trainers' thoughtful questions might play a crucial role in enhancing teachers' higher level cognitive processes; hence the importance of planning effective probing questions. Teachers who experience this kind of cognitive exercise will then become more empowered to argue about their decisions, more informed to influence their practice, and be better prepared to pose the same type of questions to their language learners. In other words, trainers should ask the difficult questions, appeal to scaffolding techniques on a regular basis, and expect deeper conclusions from trainees in order to get teachers to become more critical, aware and autonomous, and also to provide trainees with a model of how to trigger critical thinking.

When receiving feedback of any kind, teachers need to be made aware of the importance of seeking evidence, closely examining reasoning and assumptions, analysing basic concepts, and tracing out implications. Unfortunately, feedback from teacher educators can often be too short or too prescriptive. Some trainers often focus on providing teachers with easy-to-implement techniques and demand that they work by the book—following steps without necessarily understanding the underlying principles of what they are doing. If we want teachers who can think critically, we first need to revisit our own processes and goals for feedback. Critical thinking needs to be an integral part of professional development and trainers have to constantly reflect upon their role in turning teachers into more critical professionals who are then able to make well-informed decisions and explain why these decisions were made.

In summary, we can say that our experience has helped us gather the following advice regarding feedback in teacher education:

- There are formal and informal moments of feedback; they are both equally powerful and strategic.

- When observing a lesson, do not postpone the feedback session until it is too late; whether it will be given immediately after the lesson or the following day, it is important that teachers still remember what happened in class.
- Write your own probing questions before the feedback moment, focusing on the profile of the teacher, your goals as a trainer and the institutional objectives.
- Choose your words appropriately and carefully.
- Base your comments on evidence, illustrating your feedback with instances of what really happened, what was said and done.
- Engage the teacher in critical thinking, getting them to justify their decisions and appeal to a more concrete explanation of what they had planned to do and what actually happened.
- Help the teacher come up with a tangible plan of action.
- Adopt a professional and objective discourse.
- Strike a balance between assertiveness and support, feeding and leading.
- Develop trust by acknowledging teachers' needs.
- Have a holistic view of the teacher.

References:

Bax, S. (1997) Roles for a teacher-educator in context-sensitive teacher education. *ELT Journal*, Volume 51/3. Oxford University Press.

Brookfield, S. (1987). *Developing Critical Thinking: Challenging Adults to Explore Alternative Ways of Thinking and Acting*. San Francisco: Jossey-Bass.

Brown, H. D. (2004). Some practical thoughts about student-sensitive critical pedagogy. *The Language Teacher*. 28 (7): 23-27.

Ennis, R. H. (2003). Critical thinking assessment. In Fasko, Dan (Ed.), *Critical thinking and reasoning: Current theories, research, and practice*. Cresskill, NJ: Hampton.

Freeman, D. (1989) Teacher Training, Development, and Decision Making: A Model of Teaching and Related Strategies for Language Teacher Education. In *TESOL Quarterly* Volume 23, number 1, March.

King, A. (1995). Designing the instructional process to enhance critical thinking across the curriculum. *Teaching of Psychology*, 22(1), 13–17.

Knowles, M. S., Swanson, R. A., & Holton, E. F. III (2005). *The adult learner: The definitive classic in adult education and human resource development* (6th ed.). San Francisco: Elsevier Science and Technology Books.

National School Reform Faculty (2002). http://www.nsrfharmony.org/system/files/protocols/probing_questions_guide.pdf.

Taba, H. (1966). *Teaching strategies and cognitive functioning in elementary school children*. Cooperative Research Project, No. 2404. San Francisco: San Francisco State College.

Wallace, S. & Gravells, J. (2007) *Mentoring, Second Edition*. Exeter: Learning Matters.

William, D. (2011) *Embedded Formative Assessment*. Bloomington: Solution Tree Press.

Tasks for Chapter 5

One of the greatest challenges in the life of a trainer is to instill an environment of trust and constant feedback. Everyone seems to ask for and expect more feedback, yet very few will be genuinely open to it or even act as protagonists of their careers, actively asking people for input. It is not an easy or natural task, asking for someone's opinion or evaluation of you and your work, but it is an essential part of career development. It might be a little painful at times, but if you want to promote this kind of interaction among the people you work with, you should definitely take the first step.

First, we need to understand that the general question, "How am I doing?" won't get us very far. It usually triggers a simplified, one-word answer. When asking for feedback, it seems more effective to specifically ask about the good and the bad. You can ask "What are some things that I did well?" and "What are some things I could have done differently or better?" Whenever possible, ask for details and examples. This will better illustrate the feedback being given and hopefully ensure that you have a better idea of what steps to take and how to improve. It is also important to find a balance and ask both open-ended questions and specific ones. Some possible questions are:

1. What specifically can I do to become a more effective teacher / teacher trainer?
2. Who should I be working with more closely?
3. Which parts of my style concern you the most?
4. What can I learn from the people I work with?
5. What behaviours do you think might prevent me from being a better professional?

You should always remember to keep an open mind and accept feedback graciously. Feedback is a gift and like any gift you receive you are entitled to do whatever you find more appropriate with it: keep it, use it, throw it away, swap it for something else, or ignore it entirely. But whatever you choose to do, always say thank you, and try not to get defensive. Even if you do not agree with them, or decide not to follow their advice, acknowledge that giving feedback is also hard and these people are trying to help you develop.

Another point you want to bear in mind is that you do not just work with your boss, so it is important to make sure the feedback you are seeking out is well rounded. Approach all sorts of people. Speak to your boss, reach out to fellow teachers, engage with your students, and even discuss your strengths and weaknesses with family and friends.

Task 1

Choose three people that you would like to receive feedback from. One of them should be acting or have acted as your immediate superior (a former teacher, trainer, or supervisor). The second one should be a peer. And the third one should be somebody who is not in your professional circle. Approach each one of them and clearly explain your objectives. Tell them that as part of your professional development programme, you would like them to give you honest feedback that might help you become a full-fledged teacher trainer. Schedule a day and allow them some time to organise their thoughts and observe you more closely. Then remember to welcome what they say, ask for examples and ask for advice. Write everything down and after talking to the three people, analyse your notes and try to identify how their input is similar to your own perceptions. Finally use the table below to devise an action plan for your own individual development. Consider what the feedback has helped you identify as a priority and plan specific actions to develop a certain knowledge, enhance a skill, or change your attitude. Then, consider obstacles that might prevent you from implementing these actions (e.g., lack of time) and how you plan to overcome these.

Professional Objective: _____

Area to improve (knowledge/skill/attitude)	Actions to improve this knowledge/skill/attitude	Start:	Finish:	Possible Obstacles	How to overcome these obstacles

One of the most difficult things in the work of a teacher educator is to find feedback on our performance.

Task 2

One of the most difficult things in the work of a teacher educator is to find feedback on our performance. The activity of supervising teachers' development can be quite lonely and we often lack feedback on what we do. For instance, unless a more experienced trainer shadows a feedback session, we might depend on our own assessment of how effective our feedback sessions are (together with teachers' feedback, naturally) to determine steps for development.

In this task, you will need to record a feedback session with a teacher you are currently working with. If you are not acting as a trainer yet, ask a colleague to welcome you into their classroom and schedule a feedback session with them. During the feedback, record everything that you say. Remember to ask for the teacher's permission to do so. Then, it is time to analyse the interaction. You can either listen to the recording alone or invite an experienced trainer to listen to it with you. As you listen to the recording, consider the following:

1. The nature of the questions asked:

   a. Did I ask enough probing questions?
   b. Did I ask too many probing questions?
   c. Did my questions allow the teacher to explain their intentions and expand?
   d. Could I have reworded my questions to sound more encouraging?
   e. Did I guide too much with my questions or was there plenty of room for reflection?
   f. Did I sound scripted or did I interact with the teacher in a more organic manner?

2. The type of answers given:

   a. Did I accept justifications that had no solid basis or theoretical foundation?
   b. Was the teacher answering the questions or avoiding them?
   c. Could I have asked more follow-up questions to clarify what the teacher said?

> If you are not acting as a trainer yet, ask a colleague to welcome you into their classroom and schedule a feedback session with them.

3. The teacher's reactions:

   a. Did the teacher sound comfortable and relaxed?
   b. Did the teacher ever seem hurt or offended by what I said?
   c. Did the teacher feel that their stage of professional development was being respected (treating a novice teacher as someone less experienced or interacting with a more senior teacher acknowledging their background and qualifications)?

4. The kind of input provided:

   a. Was my input coherent and logical?
   b. Did I justify my advice using both my experience and sound theoretical background?
   c. Did I give the teacher alternatives for their practice?
   d. Was I clear and convincing?
   e. Did I make assumptions about the teacher's actions or did I allow them to justify what happened?
   f. Did I manage to focus on facts and provide examples of what was said and done?

Chapter 6

Promoting continuous professional development

"Based on our experience, although we make a conscious effort to try and trigger more holistic reflection (development) instead of simply providing teachers with specific techniques that have to be multiplied (training), we believe there is a time and a place for training, too. We therefore like to focus on a combination of teacher development and teacher training..."

A lot has been said about the terminology used to identify and categorise initiatives that aim at helping teachers become more effective and confident. Mann (2005), for example, articulates distinctions between the following terms: teacher training, teacher preparation, teacher education, teacher development, professional development, continuing professional development (CPD), and staff development. In order to narrow down the scope of our work, we have chosen to limit the contrast to two key concepts: "professional development" and "training." Mann goes on to define "training" as an introduction to methodological choices and a familiarisation of concepts and terms, and "development" as a process that is career oriented and more inclusive of personal and moral dimensions. From our experience we prefer to try, whenever possible, to favour an approach towards development rather than more formalised initiatives that aim at training—though we do not believe training is necessarily negative, as some will argue. Edge (2003), for example, states that "to train is to instill habits or skills, and the word collocates just as happily with dogs and seals as with teachers." We think the dichotomy is not necessarily so black and white.

Based on our experience, although we make a conscious effort to try and trigger more holistic reflection (development) instead of simply providing teachers with specific techniques that have to be multiplied (training), we believe there is a time and a place for training, too. We therefore like to focus on a combination of teacher development and teacher training as defined by Ur (1998). In other words: provide a developmental process that aims at the whole person in an ongoing mode, stressing the importance of reflection and meaningfulness of content—as in teacher development— but also add elements of teacher training to the scheme to provide the necessary organisation and avoid the "pooling of ignorance" (as mentioned by her). We believe that a certain balance between development and training, as well as the flexibility required to implement them, are essential when faced with a wide range of profiles of teachers. In this book, we would like to encourage teacher educators to consider, as much as possible, a broader perspective of professional growth, as presented by Johnston (2003) who aims at raising teachers' consciousness of personal values in order to relate them to the decisions made in teaching, without promptly overlooking the possible benefits of attempts to implement training on given occasions.

A lot of discussions and research have been carried out regarding the importance of making professional development a continuous process and the positive impact of action research. As obvious as it may seem, the challenge lies in how one can engage

> ...it is very important to take into consideration the profile of the teachers you are working with, your institutional goals and targets, and your own objectives.

fellow teachers in a never-ending cycle of learning. In order to systematically promote this, we suggest teacher educators establish an environment of experimentation amongst the staff via the implementation of ongoing action research. Teachers should be constantly encouraged to engage in a variety of projects in order to research different areas of their practice until the curiosity and willingness to experiment become second nature. Burns (2005), for example, emphasises the importance of action research as a tool to generate learning. According to her, action research is clearly a "vehicle for practitioners'" personal and professional development, and it has played an important part in putting the teacher at the centre of efforts to understand and develop language teaching and learning practice.

Nevertheless, other actions geared towards professional development can also be encouraged so as to promote a continuous desire to grow professionally. Teacher educators can call upon other reflective and developmental processes that can be combined with action research or not. These ideas include reflective practice (Nunan 1989), action learning (Zuber-Skerritt 1992; McGill & Beattie 1995), practitioner research (Middlewood et al 1999), and exploratory teaching (Allwright & Bailey 1991). In order to engage in these processes, teachers have appealed to varied procedures, such as peer observation (Good & Brophy 1987) and journal writing (Gebhard 1999). We do not intend to delve into such a variety of tools and techniques, but rather highlight the number of possibilities that are known today. Regardless of your choice, it is very important to take into consideration the profile of the teachers you are working with, your institutional goals and targets, and your own objectives. Deciding how continuous professional development will be encouraged is not an easy task and the outcome will depend on how aware you are of your given context and the alternatives that have been researched and experimented with.

But why does it sound so challenging to promote genuine continuous professional development? Looking at how Mann (2005) organises key themes to inform discussions about professional development, one might claim that it is not a concrete process at all. There is indeed the possibility that this complexity will prevent an institution from perceiving more immediate and tangible impact—especially because professional development should be seen more as a process than as an event. He claims, for instance, that it: (1) is a bottom–up process and as such can be contrasted with top–down staff development programmes; (2) values the insider view rather than the outsider view; (3) is independent of the organisation but often functioning more successfully with its support and recognition; (4) is a continuing process of becoming and can never be finished; (5) is a process of articulating an inner world of conscious choices made in response to the outer world of the teaching context; (6) is wider than professional growth and includes personal, moral, and value dimensions; (7) can be encouraged and integrated in both training and education programmes. We believe that when one starts getting involved in teacher education, the considerations above might seem to lack pragmatics, sounding almost ethereal—however theoretically sound they are.

One of the challenges of implementing a programme of continuous professional development is that most of the ideas, processes, and procedures mentioned above rely essentially on the teachers' willingness and abilities to self-direct. Because of this, teacher educators might feel tied-up when being pressed for better results—especially when faced with the fact that professional development is indeed a long-term process. From our experience, a strategy to expedite this process and promote more immediate results is to increase teachers' level of commitment by involving them as much as possible in the decision-making process. Zeichner (2001), for instance, suggests that teachers should be challenged to organise, formulate, and define their own objectives, assuming responsibility for their own practice, and not just take a passive role in teaching (by translating knowledge and theories into practice). We can therefore get teachers to choose what they want/need to develop and challenge them to devise action plans to achieve the objectives they themselves have set.

Looking at all the points we made above, we seem to be looking at the following context:

1. We understand that simply imposing training on teachers and forcing them to engage in courses will not be very productive, so it is important to allow teachers to choose and to show them the positive outcomes of developing professionally.
2. Research shows little impact in training initiatives that are fully managed by the institutions and forced upon teachers, so the more teachers participate in the decision-making process, the more likely they are to actually improve.
3. We believe that professional development and teacher training are not necessarily mutually excluding concepts and might be combined on certain occasions depending on the profile of teachers, teacher educators and the institution.
4. Professional Development has proven to be the best approach (but not the only one) to enhance teaching but is mainly managed by the teachers themselves and should be an ongoing process—representing a continuous long-term investment—with results that might be hard to measure.
5. Continuous Professional Development can be implemented through several actions, projects, and ideas (some of which were briefly mentioned above), but it is up to the teacher educator to study them and decide which one best suits the needs of the teachers they are working with.

Looking at this context, we can say that in order to promote professional development, the institution (or trainer) needs to provide varied and solid initiatives. A possible framework of professional development aims at helping teachers develop (1) a better understanding of foreign language acquisition, (2) a deepening of their knowledge of the teaching and the learning of English and (3) a broadening of their methodological repertoire. If we look at these three objectives, it is easy to say that effective Continuous Professional Development cannot overlook language competence as an underlying continuous focus. Even if teachers are proficient in the language, we suggest language-awareness-raising tasks be an integral component of any initiative. Cullen (1993), for instance, says we should ensure that all the components of any programme are conducted in English. As artificial as it may sound in a foreign language context (in which both teachers and trainers most likely share the same language), teacher educators need to make an effort to constantly provide teachers with opportunities to use the target language naturally. So we believe it is vital that every interaction happens in English.

Still in the realm of Continuous Professional Development, but broadening the aims so that we go beyond the three objectives mentioned above (understanding of foreign language acquisition, knowledge of the teaching and the learning of English, and methodological repertoire), we think it is very important that teacher educators consider other foci. The primary focus tends to be on developing knowledge and skills because they are more trainable (Freeman, 1989). However, we would like to suggest attention to attitude and awareness should underlie all the training initiatives. Teacher trainers tend to be more comfortable giving feedback on the actual teaching than addressing other professional issues that can be as impactful as classroom techniques. Rinvolucri (1994, p. 288) states that feedback is central to any kind of learner-centred teaching; so transparent feedback needs to be given to teachers on all the four competencies: knowledge and skills, but also on attitude and awareness.

Padwad & Dixit (2011) state:

> "[The] narrow view considers CPD (Continuous Professional Development) as the imparting/acquiring of some specific sets of skills and/or knowledge in order to deal with some specific new requirements. The broad view considers CPD as a much deeper, wider, and longer term process, in which professionals continuously enhance not only their knowledge and skills, but also their thinking, understanding and maturity; they grow not only as professionals, but also as persons; their development is not restricted to their work roles, but may also extend to new roles and responsibilities."

We truly believe an effective teacher educator can strike a healthy balance between teacher training and continuous professional development, and can follow a broader view of the latter—working towards the holistic development of professionals, helping them become better at devising tasks and using teaching

Continuous Professional Development is only effective when the teacher educator understands that teachers are different...

techniques, but also helping them understand their roles, responsibilities and attitudes towards the students, themselves, their peers, the institution, and the profession.

The kinds of tasks and activities used to promote Continuous Professional Development need to be carefully taken into account. Woodward (2003), for example, reinforces the importance of experiencing situations when she says that experiential learning is regarded as a very useful tool in English Language teacher training. Therefore, we suggest the tasks always resemble real-life situations and teachers be encouraged to put themselves in the students' shoes, discuss, engage in hands-on activities, and reflect upon actual practice. Another key element that needs to be considered in all decisions regarding the design of professional development programs is the relevance of the topics offered. As Bailey says (2006), if the supervisor focuses on an issue that is not important to the teacher, he or she may not be able to process the information provided.

Continuous Professional Development is only effective when the teacher educator understands that teachers are different and they cannot appeal to them with the same techniques and approaches, disregarding the profile of the professionals they are working with. We like to consider the choices available to an advisor, as suggested by Gebhard (1999) in Randall & Thornton (2001, p. 62):

- Directive supervision – with less experienced teachers;
- Alternative supervision – with less experienced teachers who show initiative and willingness to reflect;
- Collaborative supervision – with more qualified and experienced teachers who have the knowledge and repertoire to contribute;
- Non-directive supervision – with very qualified or resistant teachers;
- Creative supervision – adaptable to any kind of teacher; and
- Self-help-explorative supervision – with reflective teachers.

This seniority and flexibility to adapt are essential features for the success of a Continuous Professional Development programme. As McGrath (1997) states, "It goes without saying that variety in trainer training as well as in teacher training and teaching is a good thing.... To achieve particular purposes certain means will be more suitable than others." Teachers have very different profiles and therefore quite diverse needs. Richards and Farrell (2005) talk about the importance of understanding what is meant by teacher development from the perspective of novice teachers and expert teachers. They refer to Berliner (1987), who claims that experienced teachers know what typical classroom activities and expected problems and solutions are like. By comparison, novice teachers are less familiar with the subject matter, teaching strategies, and teaching contexts. This difference alone would require different approaches to the staff, according to how aware they are of what goes on in their practice. Development initiatives then should vary from a more elementary approach to teaching (more prescriptive) to a more complex perspective (more reflective) according to the teacher under one's supervision.

Nevertheless, as surprising as it may seem, Hall & Simeral (2008, p. 16) claim that "it is commonly believed that because one works in the realm of education, one is open to learning new things. Unfortunately, this is not always the case. Often, educators are even more resistant to tackling something new, which is ironic, really, when one of the primary purposes of education is to teach students to value learning." Therefore, the challenge lies in getting teachers to embrace professional development in a genuine manner. However, both Fullan (2014) and Hall & Simeral (2008) also reinforce the effectiveness of peer collaboration and the power within creating learning communities. The challenge is then to strike a balance between opening up to teachers' free initiative to identify their own training needs, and acting as an instructional leader (Fullan, 2014) suggesting and guiding more assertively considering the results and the needs of the school.

From an individual perspective, teachers have to develop subject-matter knowledge, pedagogical expertise, self-awareness, understanding of learners, and understanding of curriculum and materials and career advancement. Professional Development needs can be identified autonomously through self-reflection, conversations with superiors, the analysis of satisfaction surveys and the reading of lesson observation reports. However, "teachers' skills and knowledge sometimes become outdated or there may be a lack of fit between the knowledge and skills the teacher possesses and what the school needs" (Richards and Farrell, 2005).

In summary, we believe that the following nine features should underlie Continuous Professional Development initiatives:

1. Teacher involvement – Only if teachers are truly involved in the process will professional development be continuous and real. It is important to create communities and allow everyone to take responsibility.
2. Long-Term and holistic development – Professionals are encouraged to consider their roles and responsibilities continuously.
3. Indirect language work – Proficiency is developed marginally and English is the only authorised language in all interactions.
4. Constant feedback – Teachers are constantly informed of their strengths and weaknesses in knowledge, skills, attitude, and awareness.
5. Relevance – Topics, dynamics, structures, and priorities that are perceived by teachers as meaningful
6. Andragogical principles – Teachers are adults and adults learn differently.
7. Experiential learning – Experiential learning and loop input are privileged.
8. Varied techniques – In order to cater to the very eclectic profile of teachers, trainers need to resort to a wide range of techniques and strategies.
9. Balance between individual and institutional needs – Professionals' needs to be catered to as well as the institutions' goals.

References:

Allwright, D. & Bailey, K. (1991) *Focus on the Language Classroom: an Introduction to Classroom Research for Language Teachers*. New York: Cambridge University Press.

Bailey, Kathleen. (2006). *Language Teacher Supervision*. Cambridge: CUP.

Beaven, B. (2004) *How Eight English Language Teacher Trainers Made the Transition From Teaching to Training*. Unpublished dissertation. Exeter: The University of Exeter.

Berliner, D. C. (1987). Ways of thinking about students and classrooms by more and less experienced teachers (pp 60-83). In J. Calderhead (Ed.), *Exploring teachers' thinking*. London: Cassell.

Burns, A. (2005) Action Research: an evolving paradigm? *Language Teaching*, 38.2, 57-54.

Cullen, R. (1993) Incorporating a Language Improvement Component in Teacher Training Programmes. In *ELT Journal*, volume 48. Oxford Journals.

Edge, J. (2003) *Teacher Development (MSc TESOL Module)*. Birmingham: Aston University.

Fullan, M. (2014) *The Principal—Three Keys to Maximizing Impact*. San Francisco: Jossey-Bass.

Freeman, D. (1989) Teacher Training, Development, and Decision Making: A Model of Teaching and Related Strategies for Language Teacher Education. In *TESOL Quarterly*, Volume 23, number 1, March.

Gebhard, J. (1999) Reflecting through a Teaching Journal. In Gebhard & Oprandy. *Language Teaching Awareness*, 78-98. Cambridge: Cambridge University Press.

Good, T. L. & Brophy, J. E. (1987) *Looking in Classrooms, 3rd edition.* New York: Harper & Row.

Hall, P. & Simeral, A. (2008) *Building Teachers' Capacity for Success—a Collaborative Approach for Coaches and School Leaders.* Alexandria: Association for Supervision and Curriculum Development.

Johnston, B. (2003) *Values in English Language Teaching.* Mahwah: Lawrence Erlbaum.

Mann, S. (2005) The Language Teacher's Development. *Language Teaching*, 38, pp 103-118. Cambridge University Press.

McGill, I. & Beattie, L. (1995) *Action learning,* 2nd edition. London: Kogan Page.

McGrath, I. (1997) Feeding, Leading, Showing, Throwing: Process choices in teacher training and trainer training. In McGrath (ed). *Learning to train: Perspectives on the Development of Language Teacher Trainers.* Hemel Hempstead: Prentice Hall, in association with the British Council.

Middlewood, D., Coleman, M. & Lumby, J. (1999) *Research in Education: Making a Difference.* London: Paul Chapman Publishing.

Nunan, D. (1989) *Understanding Language Classrooms; a guide for teacher-initiated action.* Englewoods Cliffs: Prentice-Hall.

Padwad, A. & Dixit, K. (2011) *Continuing Professional Development: An annotated bibliograpgy.* In: www.britishcouncil.org.in. <accessed on November 2nd, 2012: http://www.britishcouncil.org/cpdbiblio.pdf>

Randall, M. & Thornton, B. (2001) *Advising and supporting teachers.* Cambridge: Cambridge University Press.

Richards J. C. & Farrell, T. S. C. (2005) *Professional Development for Language Teachers.* New York: Cambridge University Press.

Rinvolucri, M. (1994) Key Concepts in ELT—Feedback. In *ELT Journal,* Volume 48/3. Oxford University Press.

Ur, P. (1998) Distinctions & Dichotomies—Teacher Training, Teacher Development. In *English Teaching Professional*, Issue 8—page 21.

Woodward, T. (2003) Loop Input. *ELT Journal,* 57/3 July, Oxford University Press.

Zeichner, K. M. (2001, November). *Educating reflective teachers for learner-centered education: Possibilities and contradictions.* Lecture presented at the National Conference of College Professors of English as a Foreign Language. Londrina, Brazil.

Zubber-Skerritt, O. (1992) *Improving Learning and Teaching through Action Learning and Action Research.* Presented at the Higher Education RDSA Conference, University of Queensland.

Tasks for Chapter 6

Pursuing Continuous Professional Development (CPD) can be both challenging and exciting. It is an activity that needs to be initiated, supervised, and revisited by each professional, and should not rely on external motivators. Schools, companies, and organisations can provide teachers and trainers with opportunities to learn and grow, but each individual needs to take responsibility for their career. So, one of the most effective things one can do to ensure continuous learning is to devise a long-term plan of development. Trainers can help teachers identify their gaps and possibilities to grow and brainstorm which initiatives will help them achieve their goals faster. Likewise, trainers should never turn a blind eye to their own development, and ought to keep on looking for new ways of enhancing their knowledge, skills, attitude, and awareness.

Task 1

Many things can be done autonomously in order to avoid the "pooling of ignorance" mentioned by Ur (1998). Look at the list of professional development choices below and check the corresponding boxes:

	I already do this	I would like to give it a try	I won't do this because...
Developing my own lexical book			
Visiting websites on EFL matters			
Writing a blog			
Writing a journal			
Joining an online discussion list			
Joining a Teacher's Association			
Teaching a new level or a different age group			
Starting an independent study group			
Attending a conference			

Presenting at a conference			
Carrying out some kind of action research			
Recording and analysing my own lessons			
Asking learners for specific feedback on my lessons			
Coaching a colleague			
Doing peer observations			
Asking a peer to observe me			
Doing an online course			
Writing an article for an international magazine/journal			
Writing my own materials			
Taking a course for English teachers			
Studying for an international teaching award			
Taking a course on other subjects (e.g., Education, Psychology, Management)			

Task 2

Genuine professional development can only be achieved if one is fully aware of their strengths and weaknesses. Part of devising a solid action plan relies on the ability to prioritise learnings and delve into areas that deserve more immediate attention, despite being more or less appealing. Oftentimes some of our weaknesses only exist because they relate to knowledge or skills that we are not particularly interested in. The first step to work on these competences and develop them needs to be a step towards a greater level of awareness of what we like and do not like, what we know and what we do not know. After learning more about our professional persona we can decide how to invest time and energy in something that may not attract us.

We have selected some (and only some) areas of knowledge that a language teacher might find relevant. Study the table below and asses how you feel about each of these areas and how familiar you are with them.

Then, select two or three areas that you would like to learn more about and devise a plan on how you intend to improve your knowledge and how you will measure whether you have actually improved. You can revisit this table (and add other areas to it) on a regular basis or whenever you finish a course, for example.

		How I feel about it			How much I know about it			
		I don't really like it	It's ok	I love it	I don't know enough about it	I know just enough about it	I know it very well	I have it
Foreign Language Acquisition	How different languages connect in the mind							
	Age and language learning (the idea of a "critical period")							
	Learning words in a second/foreign language							
	Universal grammar							
	What is interlanguage?							
	Discourse analysis							
	Literacy							
	Communication strategies							
	Phonology							
Knowledge of the Teaching and Learning of English	Lesson Planning							
	Materials and Resources							
	Teaching Speaking							
	Teaching Writing							
	Teaching Listening							
	Teaching Reading							
	Teaching Grammar							
	Teaching Lexis							
	Teaching Pronunciation							

Teaching Discourse								
Testing and Assessment								
Teaching Learners with Special Needs								
Using technology								
Grammar Translation								
The Direct Method								
The Audio-Lingual Method								
The Silent Way								
Suggestopedia								
Total Physical Response (TPR)								
The Communicative Approach								
Task Based Learning (TBL)								
Presentation, Practice, Production (PPP)								
Test-Teach-Test (TTT)								
The Lexical Approach								
Dogme								
Content and Language Integrated Learning (CLIL)								

The rows from "Grammar Translation" downward are grouped under the vertical label **Methodological Repertoire**.

> Experiential learning can be defined as the process of learning through experience, the process of learning through reflection on doing.

Task 3

In Chapter 6, we mentioned the effectiveness of using experiential learning principles when developing teachers. Experiential learning can be defined as the process of learning through experience, the process of learning through reflection on doing. In this kind of approach, the teacher does not have a passive role and needs to participate actively in activities in order to reflect upon the experience they had. Even though the idea of getting people to do things to learn better is not at all new, it was at the beginning of the 1970s that David A. Kolb (1983) helped to develop the modern theory of Experiential Learning. He drew heavily on the work of John Dewey, Kurt Lewin, and Jean Piaget, and came up with a cycle similar to the one below:

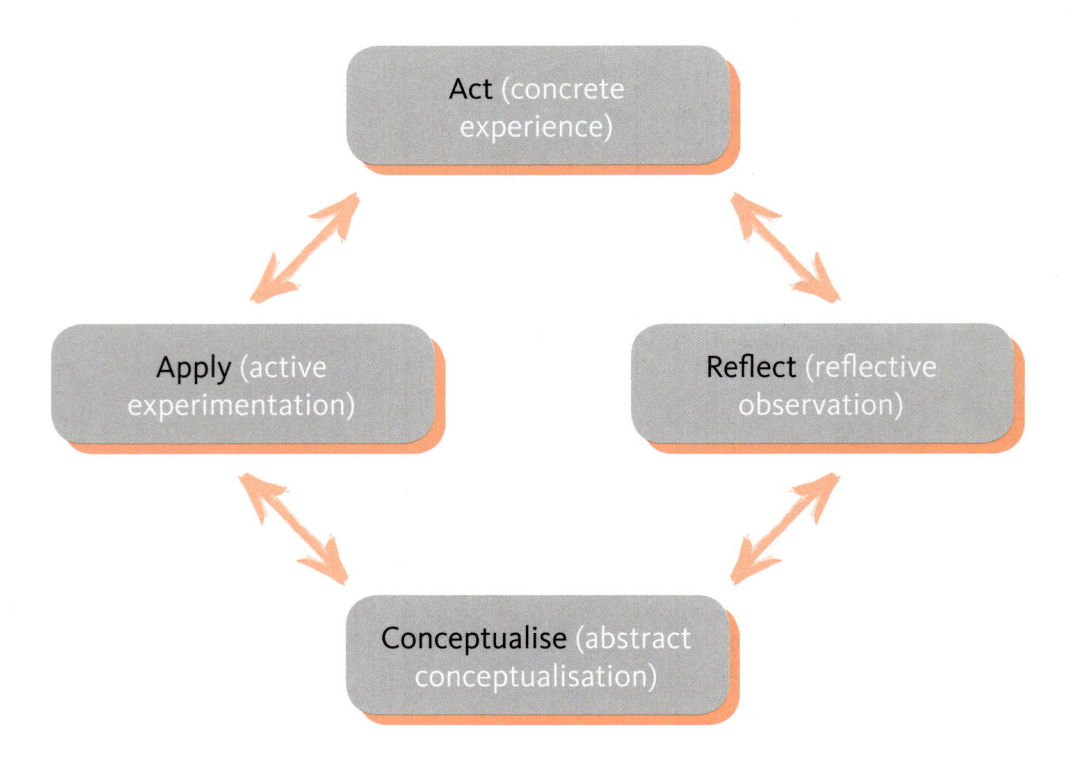

Act (concrete experience)

Reflect (reflective observation)

Conceptualise (abstract conceptualisation)

Apply (active experimentation)

> ...the teacher does not have a passive role and needs to participate actively in activities in order to reflect upon the experience they had...

Considering the Experiential Learning Cycle and the idea that people might learn better if they are given the opportunity to go through an experience and then discuss it, how would you plan a workshop/session to help teachers understand the ideas below?

1. Jig-saw reading
2. Bottom-up and Top-down strategies for listening
3. Test-Teach-Test approach
4. Using Cuisenaire rods
5. Understanding the affective filter of elementary adult learners
6. Integrating Skills
7. Using flashcards
8. Understanding the difference between test validity and reliability

References:

Kolb, D. A. (1983). *Experiential Learning: experience as the source of learning and development.* New Jersey: Prentice Hall.

Ur, P. (1998) Distinctions & Dichotomies—Teacher Training, Teacher Development. In *English Teaching Professional*, Issue 8—page 21.

Chapter 7

The art of coaching

"We have tried to formalise teacher training as much as possible by referring to some of the research and science behind it because we truly believe that a lot of what happens nowadays is casual, erratic, and feeble. However, as much as we attempt to bring teacher education closer to a more pragmatic and scientific perspective, there is still an element of art in this career that cannot be overlooked. In this last chapter, we would like to share some of our very own perceptions of how coaching other professionals might have traces of an art."

© Seroldo/Shutterstock.com

We have already discussed the challenges that a teacher educator might face, raised issues regarding lesson observations, systematised process choices for teacher training programs, analysed types of supervision, addressed continuous professional development, and suggested some principles for effective feedback moments. We have tried to formalise teacher training as much as possible by referring to some of the research and science behind it because we truly believe that a lot of what happens nowadays is casual, erratic, and feeble. However, as much as we attempt to bring teacher education closer to a more pragmatic and scientific perspective, there is still an element of art in this career that cannot be overlooked. In this last chapter, we would like to share some of our very own perceptions of how coaching other professionals might have traces of an art.

As teachers, teacher trainers, teacher educators, supervisors, pedagogical coordinators, or academic managers/directors, we are constantly faced with a fairly good dose of emotion. It is part of our daily lives, whether we work with toddlers, senior citizens, elementary adult learners, or primary school teachers. So no wonder teaching is often described as an art, a vocation, or a calling. As much as we feel that this label does not help the career—because it seems to under-estimate the pragmatic value of professionalism and over-romanticise a very serious job—we feel we have to agree that one can easily relate images of passionate commitment, inspirational lessons, and life-changing experiences to teachers and educators. Countless accounts of unique teachers and professors have been turned into best-sellers and blockbusters. Tears and laughter have been triggered by poems, novels, movies and songs that describe the intensity of the life of a teacher and our relationship with students. Developing teachers, therefore, cannot be very different. There is the natural need for systematic approaches and very rational decisions, but there are also instances of profound poetry, a touch of magic and talent that could justify the theme of this chapter: coaching as an art.

Under no circumstance are we implying that someone who works with the development of teachers is an artist. Nor are we trying to encourage the mistaken idea that coaching, teacher development, and teacher education is a random act (not necessarily professional) to be carried out by a few gifted souls. Art can be defined as the expression or application of human creative skill and imagination, producing works to be appreciated primarily for their beauty or emotional power. In this definition we can easily identify which features of "art" can be immediately associated with coaching. Coaching teachers will indeed demand creativity and a lot of imagination. It is an activity that does not

> Art can be defined as the expression or application of human creative skill and imagination, producing works to be appreciated primarily for their beauty or emotional power.

rely on routinised and predictable actions. It revolves around dealing with the unexpected, adapting to each individual, constantly shifting paradigms, and appealing to new ideas and plans. Imagination and flexibility are vital to the work of a teacher trainer or coach.

Nonetheless, the outcome of such activity is not limited to beautiful or emotional products—even though these might also come about among many other outcomes. The process is much more relevant, powerful, and important than the final product itself, and because of that, trainers have to be able to take a long-term view. The beautiful and emotional conclusion (intrinsic outcome in a work of art) may never be seen by the coach or trainer. Even though we should see ourselves as catalysts of change, we should also be patient and philosophical. After all, we will not necessarily be there to see the results of the coaching that we have done. Actual results may not happen for some time—as opposed to an artistic expression that is unlikely not to generate something that people can see, listen to, feel, and/or appreciate. Trainers, unlike artists, need to understand that positive outcomes—when and if they come—may also be quite different from those intended.

Coaching a professional is more than simply providing teachers with a set of tools or a list of activities and techniques; there needs to be a commitment to actually influencing lives and promoting change. The ability to help people revisit their own beliefs and wish to be better individuals, in our opinion, is the side of our work that presents features of art. After all, it aims at bringing a beautiful final product to surface. Features of art but not an art in itself: since the intentions of helping people change may not be translated into a concrete outcome.

We believe that some of the characteristics that a trainer needs to display in order to better perform this part of their professional activity and add elements of art to professional development are:

* Trainers need to display skills of empathy and understanding: These skills have to be deployed consciously and need to be constantly developed. Like an artist who develops a more careful analysis of the world around them and whose sensitivity adds further value to their work, a teacher educator should also become an attentive observer of human nature, learning how

> Good artists are always studying, reading, and learning, and are able to use a wide range of techniques to communicate a more subjective message.

to respect, sympathise with, and understand the challenges, fears, and dreams of their coachees.

- **Trainers need to have facilitation skills and should help people refine their thinking:** Coaching others is not about providing people with ready-made answers. It is not about offering recipes or showing all your knowledge. It is about guiding people to discover their own perspective. Different art-lovers will see different things in the same painting. A song will trigger different emotions according to people's background and life experiences. Likewise, a coach should encourage teachers to find their own connection with students, materials, lessons, and the language. Coaches should guide coachees through this process, facilitating their discoveries in a more critical and refined manner.

- **Trainers need to have an up-to-date knowledge of the literature and should systematically relate it to their very own practical knowledge:** Good artists are always studying, reading, and learning, and are able to use a wide range of techniques to communicate a more subjective message. However, they always seem to use this technical and formal knowledge as a springboard for their own life experience; emotion meets technique to create feelings. Likewise, a coach is much more likely to be effective once they can strike a balance between what they have done and seen, and what they have read and learned. Memorising theories and presenting them in a lecture is as ineffective as simply offering advice based on what you have once done. There has got to be a clear combination of theory and practice, translated into new knowledge, deeper reflection and an organic—yet founded—development of ideas. In summary, coaches should not only be able to explain principles but also relate them to practice in a meaningful way.

- **Trainers have to focus on a long-term view:** Isolated workshops, casual observations, and seasonal sessions do not necessarily represent the work of a teacher educator. They might be part of a bigger plan, but unless they are associated with a development programme that aims at long-term goals, they become nothing more than good

> Art has inspired generations to change the way relationships are built, governments act, and people behave.

intentions. Actual professional development needs to be constantly looking into the future and be built by diverse initiatives that are carefully linked. Many artists want to find their place in history; they want future generations to learn from their work and remember their contributions to society. There is an intended message that is not limited to the here and now. Coaches should also be focusing on the impact that our actions are going to have in one, two, or ten years. Our efforts have to go beyond the quick fix; what we do has to be an investment for the years to come.

- **Trainers have to see themselves as catalysts of change:** Art has inspired generations to change the way relationships are built, governments act, and people behave. Art does not intend to authoritatively impose new paradigms. It wants to expedite change and provoke decision-makers and each individual to consider alternatives. It causes uneasiness and might give people that extra push to create something new. It brings people together to consider possible changes. Like teacher educators, it does not intend to find the answers and then spoon-feed them to others. It wants to accelerate the process of self-development.

There is a clear touch of art in coaching professionals, educating teachers, and training the language practitioner. The intended outcome of a teacher trainer's work is a professional who can continue to develop autonomously, with a greater level of independent thinking, feeling empowered to exercise their knowledge in a conscious and positive fashion. This often implies attitude change and intentional destabilisation of people, two outcomes that art can usually generate as well. Like artists, trainers may find resistance and challenge, and just like good artists, trainers will also need well-developed self-awareness and to be emotionally robust. Coaching other teachers should not be seen as a popularity contest. It is not about irresponsibly validating what people think of themselves, shying away from conflict. It is about destabilising, challenging the status quo, questioning, challenging, promoting more daring thoughts.

It is about calling upon what has been proved by research, learning the theories, studying the literature in order to revisit, consolidate, reinforce, and challenge one's own meandering experience in the classroom. It is about never leaving the classroom because it is amongst students that we learn the most. It is about never leaving the classroom because it is the most coherent way to stay closer to the teachers we are coaching.

There is indeed an artistic beauty and an emotional outcome in training teachers; there is a certain art in what we do. If we do not fall prey to the general misconception that art is for the gifted and that it is solely based on gut feeling and innate gifts, we can find very helpful associations between what we do as teachers and teacher educators and some of the most remarkable artistic outcomes of history.

• •